Fulfilling God's Call: Guidelines for Candidacy

For Deacons, Elders, and Local Pastors
The United Methodist Church

D1530141

2009 Edition

Fulfilling God's Call: Guidelines for Candidacy

For Deacons, Elders, and Local Pastors
The United Methodist Church

2009 Edition

General Board of Higher Education and Ministry
The United Methodist Church
Nashville, Tennessee

Table of Contents

Preface

Section 1. **Introduction to *Guidelines for Candidacy***

Section 2. **Beginning Candidacy**

Section 3. **Declaring Candidacy**

Section 4. **Continuing as a Certified Candidate**

Section 5. **Completing Candidacy**

Section 6. **Resources**

Preface

The *Candidacy Guidebook* has been a staple of the candidacy process since 1997. It provides information and material to guide one through the candidacy process to licensed or ordained ministry.

During periods of flux in the church's understanding and decisions about ministry leadership; in times of significant change in our disciplinary statements regarding ordering for ministry; the *Candidacy Guidebook* has given direction, encouraged exploratory reflection, and provided support for persons exploring a call to ordained or licensed ministry and candidacy mentors assigned to be their companion in the process.

The 2008 General Conference took steps to alter the candidacy process to allow for more freedom and adaptability to accommodate a broader, more diverse range of people and to expand authorized United Methodist settings out of which people can enter candidacy for ordained or licensed ministry. In this alteration this guidebook is no longer the single required resource for those going through candidacy.

> *Those beginning candidacy for licensed or ordained ministry: shall be a professing member in good standing of The United Methodist Church or a baptized participant of a recognized United Methodist campus ministry or other United Methodist ministry setting for a minimum of one (1) year. . . . After registration by the district superintendent with GBHEM, mentor and candidate will study the resources adopted by the conference board of ordained ministry.* (¶311.1, 2008 Book of Discipline)

In this change toward more flexibility, however, the standard for excellence is not diminished. The *Discipline* still encourages persons to use resources recommended by the General Board of Higher Education and Ministry (GBHEM). To that end this 2009 edition, now called *Fulfilling God's Call: Guidelines for Candidacy*, has been revised and edited to reflect the *2008 Book of Discipline* changes to the process for entering and completing candidacy and still stands as a premier guide for candidates and candidacy mentors preparing for ordained or licensed ministry in The United Methodist Church.

I want to thank the writers of the original *Candidacy Guidebook* who established the standard for candidacy guidelines: Richard Hunt, Sondra Matthaei, Robert Kohler, and Joaquin Garcia. Much of their thought and wisdom remains in this edition.

I encourage you to use this workbook in a way that adapts to your life experience, your academic background, your ministry situation, and candidacy needs.

Sincerely,

Sharon Rubey, Editor
Director, Candidacy and Conference Relations
Division of Ordained Ministry
General Board of Higher Education and Ministry

Section 1
Introduction to Guidelines for Candidacy

The Purpose of the Guidelines

As an inquiring candidate, you may have completed *The Christian as Minister* and/or *Understanding God's Call: A Ministry Inquiry Process*. You have now enrolled in candidacy for licensed or ordained ministry and the *Guidelines for Candidacy* is your guide to the rest of the candidacy process. Candidacy is your opportunity to explore many facets of the decisions you are making about your future in licensed or ordained ministry.

The *Guidelines* used in relationship with a candidacy mentor offer the opportunity for a shared safe space for exploration, discernment, and growth. *Guidelines for Candidacy* provides procedural information, requirements from *The United Methodist Book of Discipline*, thoughtful reflections and questions to guide your thinking, and a sequenced process to candidates and their candidacy mentors.

The spiritual journey that has led you to this point is lifelong. During candidacy, you will be journeying with a candidacy mentor who will help you continue to discern where God is leading. This guidebook provides a wide variety of resources so that you are able to tailor your candidacy studies to fit you. You and your candidacy mentor are encouraged to plan candidacy studies that fit your background, experience, and needs.

We invite you to begin with this prayer:

> *O God, who planned and prepared the universe for your purposes, guide me in my journey through this candidacy process so that I may discern your purposes and callings in me and in those whom I contact in my explorations. Stir me to respond so that I may fulfill your purposes in my life. Amen.*

Notes:

The early part of these *Guidelines* begins with opportunities for the candidate and candidacy mentor to get acquainted through mutual sharing of life circumstances and experience. Both candidate and mentor may talk together about their personal call to licensed or ordained ministry and together share hopes for this candidacy process.

As a **candidate** beginning this part of the journey, review the descriptions of call and discernment that you have prepared earlier.

As a **candidacy mentor**, remember again your own sense of calling and discernment.

Foundational Elements of Candidacy

Mentoring

The heart of candidacy is in spiritual discernment through shared reflection, and in the personal relationships that you establish with the persons you meet in each step of candidacy. One of the most important of these relationships will be with your candidacy mentor.

"Through the many instruments God uses to help us discern God's call, one of the most common and most important is another person. . . ." The word mentor derived from the name of the teacher of Odysseus's son in the epic poem about a life journey, Homer's *Odyssey*. *"(Mentor) has come to mean a trusted and experienced teacher, guide, counselor, or adviser." (Mentors as Instruments as God's Call*, Justo Gonzalez)

"Mentoring is distinct from the evaluative and supervisory process that is a part of preparation for ministry." (¶349.2, *Discipline*) Candidacy mentors are trained to provide counsel and guidance and to create a "safe place for reflection and growth."

Throughout your prescribed time with your candidacy mentor, you have an opportunity to discuss many issues in an informal, personalized setting. The experience intends to provide the freedom, confidentiality, flexibility, and stability that is essential for maximum growth and understanding of yourself in relation to a call to licensed or ordained ministry. From a theological perspective, this time of companionship and guidance is designed to help open you to the Holy Spirit in your decision making.

The candidacy mentor works with you as a co-discerner, consultant, and adviser to encourage and support you as you consider vocational and ministry decisions. He or she is also a representative of the church who informs and explains United Methodist understanding and accountability to the teaching and polity under which you will serve and lead as you represent and serve Christ through The United Methodist Church.

You saw above the root of 'mentor' is an experienced guide and adviser. The root of 'candidacy' is 'candid,' which means unbiased, forthright, honest, and objective. Careful attention to being candid about one's life, beliefs, and experiences in relation to future effectiveness for licensed or ordained ministry enables you to remove from your life anything that would be harmful or a stumbling block to others before you can be openly, honestly, and faithfully in ministry with them.

A Mutual Commitment

In accepting the role of a candidacy mentor, the mentor pledges to be available in your explorations and discernment and to pray for and with you. You are invited to commit yourself to explore all aspects of your spiritual calling and journey, to ask for what you need, and to pray for and with your candidacy mentor.

Commitments involve trust, honesty, and agreement. As you establish a commitment to the mentoring relationship, it is important to determine and describe how open you will be with each other and how much either person may share with others. In these ways you identify the boundaries within which you will explore topics and issues and you define the parameters of how you will honor commitment to one another throughout the candidacy process.

Confidentiality

Based on the definition of candidacy mentor and mentoring relationship above, conversations and information between you and your mentor are confidential. Only with the candidate's written permission may the candidacy mentor release details of these conversations or other personal information about the candidate. In determining a mutual commitment with one another, it is important to explore the assumptions each holds about the meaning of confidentiality and to come to agreement about parameters for sharing information with one another and outside the relationship.

Candidacy mentors have a dual primary goal to the candidate and to the church: a) to serve as a guide, consultant, and adviser to help candidates explore, discern, and determine how God is leading them to serve; b) to serve as a representative of the church in selecting faithful leaders with integrity for ministry. Both of you will need to agree on the kind of relationship that will be most helpful for the work you will do together.

- We suggest that in the first meeting together, candidate and mentor discuss and clarify agreed pledges to one another about confidentiality.

Commitments involve trust, honesty, and agreement. Both candidate and candidacy mentor commit to be available to one another; to pray for one another; and to explore together the candidate's spiritual calling and journey.

Candidacy mentors have a dual primary goal serving the candidate and the church:

a) To serve as a guide, consultant, and adviser to help candidates explore, discern, and determine how God is leading them to serve; and

b) To serve as a representative of the Church in selecting faithful leaders with integrity for ministry in the UMC.

- Include mutual expectations and plans, limitations each may have, meeting times, and deadlines.
- Part of the agreement will also be to decide together what sections of the *Guidelines for Candidacy* will benefit the most in the discernment and candidacy process and then to commit to work through each session together in a spirit of openness, honesty, and discernment.
- You can modify your agreements if necessary as candidacy progresses.

As you seek to create a mutual commitment, if either candidate or candidacy mentor discovers that yours is not a good match; then either may consult with your candidacy registrar about the situation and explore alternate possibilities.

Reflection with Your Candidacy Mentor

With your candidacy mentor, clarify any questions you have about the role of your candidacy mentor. How is the candidacy mentor your personal consultant?

Discuss the ways in which the candidacy mentor is a representative of The United Methodist Church. Discuss some ways that you represent The United Methodist Church.

Discuss what most helps you be frank and open about your life and experiences and concerns? What makes it difficult for you to be candid and fully open about your life and experiences?

Discuss the kind of relationship that will be most helpful to you, the candidate; what parts of *Guidelines* will be most beneficial; the operating assumptions held by both about confidentiality in the relationship; and the mutual understanding about the relational and reporting practices. Acknowledge a mutual commitment about these things.

Statement of Call

Your statement of call; the Weslyan historical dimensions of calling; and your statement of beliefs and understanding of United Methodist ministry are the foundational elements which will be addressed by the district committee on ordained ministry with you as they assess with you your call and gifts for ordained or licensed ministry.

God's call on your life began forming in the waters of your baptism and continues to take shape throughout your life. It is foundational to who you are as an individual; as a Christian living out your ministry in the church and in the world; and as a person exploring and declaring how God is calling you to live out that call in set-apart ministry as a licensed or ordained minister.

God's call to servant leadership is inward as it comes to the individual and outward through the discernment and validation of the church. (¶137, *Discipline*)

You will be asked to articulate your statement of call at the beginning of the candidacy process to your district superintendent and to your community of faith. It is a stance from which you will further discern and grow into increased understanding and realization.

God's call on your life began forming in the waters of your baptism and continues to take shape throughout your life. It is foundational to who you are as an individual; as a Christian living out your ministry in the church and in the world; and now, as a person exploring and declaring how God is calling you to live out that call in set-apart ministry as a licensed or ordained minister.

As a baptized member you were brought into the community of the church. There you were and continue to be formed as a member of the family of faith.

As a member of the family of faith, you became part of the church's vocation—it is called ministry. Therefore all baptized Christians are called to ministry and its derivative—service. The ministry of all Christians consists of service for the mission of God in the world. (¶132, *Discipline*)

The ministry of all Christians is shaped by the teachings of Jesus. The handing on of these teachings is entrusted to leaders who are gifted and called by God to appointed offices in the church: *some apostles, some prophets, some evangelists, some pastors and teachers, to equip the saints for the work of ministry, for building up the body of Christ* (Ephesians 4:11-12).

Whether your call has come instantly, like a sudden flash flood rushing over you, or gradually, like the rippling stream of water flowing gently over the rocks and slowly changing the shape of the rocks and perhaps the direction of the stream, it has been evolving since your baptism and you have been engaged in a discernment process. (Adapted from *Answering God's Call for Your Life*, by Robert Roth, pg. 29)

"You are not just the effect, however; you are both cause and effect. Whether you accept it or not, you always play a role in everything that happens in your life." (*Power of Wisdom*, by Aman Motwane, pg. 30)

Your vocation is bigger than your job
Which you might have to do to earn your living.
Your life is bigger than your vocation,
For work needs to be balanced by prayer and play and rest.
Your faith is bigger than your life,
as it includes others, history and creation.
The Spirit is bigger than your faith;
(the all-encompassing presence of God)
Is ever present to nourish you.

(*Answering God's Call for Your Life*, Robert Roth, pg. 25)

Wesleyan Dimensions of Calling

John Wesley's historical questions about dimensions of calling are still asked today to candidates in local church staff parish committees and in each district committee on ordained ministry to help assure that those who present themselves as candidates are "truly called of God."

Explore these questions with your candidacy mentor as you reflect on God's grace in your life and call; the gifts you bring to ministry; and your faithful response that bears the fruit of those gifts.

Grace, Gifts, and Fruit are three major dimensions of calling which come to us out of John Wesley's historical questions that he asked early "examiners" to pursue with those who were called to leadership ministry. They are closely interrelated; each connects to the other; and we look at each in the context of the others. These same questions are explored today with candidates in local church staff parish committees and in each district committee on ordained ministry, "in order that The United Methodist Church may be assured that those persons who present themselves as candidates for licensed or ordained ministry are truly called of God." (¶310, *Discipline*)

1. Do they know God as pardoning God? Have they the love of God abiding in them? Do they desire nothing but God? Are they holy in all manner of conversation?

2. Have they gifts, as well as evidence of God's grace, for the work? Have they a clear, sound understanding; a right judgment in the things of God; a just conception of salvation by faith? Do they speak justly, readily, clearly?

3. Have they fruit? Have any been truly convinced of sin and converted to God, and are believers edified by their service? (¶310, *Discipline*)

Grace is God's supreme gift of all-encompassing love active in all human life and evidenced in your call to licensed or ordained ministry. God's grace is manifested through relationship, giving new life to the recipient through the pardoning love of Jesus Christ and through the sustaining guidance of the Holy Spirit. As Christians, we greatly value God's grace as the ultimate expression of God's presence and as the foundation for gifts and fruit.

Gifts are given you by God and are the talents, abilities and skills you bring to licensed or ordained ministry and your promise for leadership. Through grace we recognize our abilities and skills and evaluate their usefulness in relationship to current and future ministries. Through grace we recognize and accept both the gifts and limitations that we have. When we know that God loves us consistently and unconditionally, we are then free to explore our gifts and limitations with openness and honesty.

Fruits are the results of God's grace made evident through our gifts. Fruit is to grace as good works is to faith in Wesleyan theology. God's grace and our faith call forth our thanksgiving and response. Jesus emphasized the relationship between sound trees and good fruit (Matthew 7:15-20, Luke 6:43-45) as a way of connecting results to their source. The source of goodness and gifts in our lives is through God's grace. What we do with what we are given can be most fully realized and demonstrated as we respond to God's grace and God's call, cultivate the gifts within us, and serve the ministry of Christ through the leadership capacity to which we are called.

Reflection with Mentor:

Describe some examples of how you have experienced the interaction between grace, gifts, and fruit in your life.

Statement of Beliefs and United Methodist Ministry

The effectiveness of the Church in mission depends on covenantal commitments between God and the ministry of all Christians, ordained and lay. *Through ordination and other offices of pastoral leadership, the Church provides for the continuation of Christ's ministry . . . . Without responsible leadership, the focus, direction, and continuity of that ministry are diminished.* (¶303.4, *Discipline*)

God's call has many manifestations and the Church cannot structure a single test of authenticity. Nevertheless, the experience of the Church and the needs of its ministry require certain qualities of faith, life, and practice from those who seek ordination as deacons and elders, (and licensing as local pastors) . . . .

In order that The United Methodist Church may be assured that those persons who present themselves as candidates for ordained and licensed ministry are truly called of God, the church expects persons seeking ordination to:
- *Communicate persuasively the Christian faith in both oral and written form . . .*
- *Be competent in the disciplines of Scripture, theology, church history, and Church polity . . .*
- *Be accountable to the United Methodist Church, accept its Doctrinal Standards and Discipline and authority. . . .* (¶304.1, *Discipline*)

Therefore, prior to being approved as a certified candidate, those wishing to pursue ordained or licensed ministry will be asked to consult with his/her mentor to provide the following written information to the district committee on ordained ministry with whom they will meet for examination.

1. The most formative experience of their Christian life
2. God's call to licensed or ordained ministry and the role of the church in their call
3. Their beliefs as a Christian
4. Their gifts for ministry
5. Their present understanding of their call to ministry as an elder, deacon, or licensed ministry
6. Their support system

(¶311.2a, *Discipline*)

The Goals and Stages of Candidacy

The Goals

Both you and the church have primary goals in this process:

For you as a candidate, the central goals are:
- to explore and discern how God is calling you to live out your call;
- to understand and complete candidacy requirements as stated in *The United Methodist Book of Discipline*, these *Guidelines*, and outlined by your annual conference; and
- to make decisions about licensed or ordained ministry.

For The United Methodist Church, through your local church or authorized United Methodist setting and your district committee on ordained ministry (dCOM), central goals of candidacy are:
- to examine your calling, gifts, and fruit as they point to your promise for effectiveness in ministry; and
- to discern how you might be part of the licensed or ordained ministry of the church.

The structure of candidacy is designed to meet both of these goals. If, at any step, you are unclear about which goal is primary, ask those involved to clarify how a procedure relates to these two basic objectives of candidacy. Keep asking until you find a satisfactory answer. Being open, honest, and mutually candid is essential for candidacy to be most helpful to you and to the church.

The Stages

There are three prescribed stages of the candidacy process:

Beginning

You began by inquiring of your local church pastor or another deacon or elder, campus minister, or the district superintendent (DS). They may have provided you with recommended resources such as *The Christian as Minister* or *Understanding God's Call: A Ministry Inquiry Process* for further discernment about call. You then submitted a statement of call to the DS and requested admission to the candidacy process. You completed an online enrollment; were assigned a candidacy mentor and were provided the resources such as the *Guidelines for Candidacy*.

Declaring Candidacy

As you study these *Guidelines* with your mentor, you will consult with the pastor or equivalent in your ministry setting, request a meeting with and a recommendation as a declared candidate from the staff parish relations committee or equivalent. If recommended, you will then meet with the charge conference or equivalent to be recommended to the district committee on ordained ministry (dCOM) who will approve you for certification at the district level. This book will tell you how to prepare for those meetings.

Certified Candidacy

Your candidacy mentor will help you know what to expect from and how to prepare to meet with the dCOM. The committee will interview, evaluate, and vote to approve you as a certified candidate. Continuation of candidacy requires annual review by your charge conference or other authorized body and renewal by the dCOM until you are licensed as a local pastor or become a provisional member of the annual conference.

Completing Candidacy

The district committee, your mentor, along with Section 5 of the *Guidelines*, will give you guidance about completing candidacy and the steps to become a provisional minister or to make another decision.

Each step in the process contributes to your preparation through developing skills, increasing competency and effectiveness, and assessing fitness and readiness. A crucial part of these steps is continuing a meaningful discernment about the specifics of God's call to you.

Taking Time for the Process to Work

You may be anxious to get through candidacy as quickly as possible. You may even look at it as just one more hurdle to get over as you proceed to licensed or ordained ministry. Remember that God moves in God's own time, so before you move too quickly and your expectations get too high, reflect for a moment on the requirements for candidacy above and in the next section below. Consider the need for adequate time to explore all the implications of the decision you and others on your behalf are about to make.

Delays can occur in the process. Some will be frustrating to you. You may have to wait weeks or months for a meeting with your faith community committee, charge conference, or dCOM. You may not be assigned to a candidacy mentor as promptly as you want, or the candidacy mentor with whom you initially work may be transferred. How you handle the frustrating aspects of candidacy may indicate how you will later handle the frustrating and unexpected challenges of a career in the bureaucratic connectional structure of The United Methodist Church.

You are urged to take responsibility for your candidacy program. Don't wait for others to ask what you want or need; to remind you of meetings; or to attend to needed details. Reach out and ask about next steps. In addition to this *Guidelines for Candidacy*, consult the *Book of Discipline* and other resources such as your candidacy mentor, pastor or district superintendent about any questions or concerns in the process. If things are not moving as you anticipated, talk with them. Find out if there is a problem. Ask for help. These frustrations and the resolution of them can be experiences for learning.

Pages 24-26 list the full requirements from the *Book of Discipline* plus a chart for your convenience.

Page 28 contains a check-off list for you to keep a record of important steps and when they are completed.

The Candidacy Process

Disciplinary Requirements for Candidacy

(¶311, *Discipline*)

¶311. *Candidacy for Licensed and Ordained Ministry*

Persons, upon hearing and heeding the call to servant leadership through licensed or ordained ministry, shall contact the pastor of their local church, clergy, or the district superintendent of the district in which their United Methodist ministry setting is located to inquire about the process of candidacy. Persons are encouraged to use resources recommended by GBHEM, such as *The Christian as Minister*, and the *Ministry Inquiry Process*.

1. Those beginning candidacy for licensed or ordained ministry:

    a) shall be a professing member in good standing of The United Methodist Church or a baptized participant of a recognized United Methodist campus ministry or other United Methodist ministry setting for a minimum of one (1) year;

    b) shall write to the district superintendent requesting admission to the candidacy process and the assignment of a candidacy mentor. Include a statement of call. Request registration through the district superintendent with GBHEM;

    c) after registration by the district superintendent with GBHEM, mentor and candidate will study the resources adopted by the conference board of ordained ministry;

    d) shall write their statement of call and responses to Wesley's historic questions in ¶310. The candidate will consult with the pastor or equivalent in ministry setting specified by the district committee on ordained ministry to request a meeting of the pastor parish relations committee or equivalent body specified by the district committee on ordained ministry to consider the statement of call and Wesley's historic questions;

    e) After approval of the candidate by pastor parish relations committee or equivalent body specified by the district committee on ordained ministry, shall meet with a charge conference or body specified by the district committee on ordained ministry called to recommend the candidate to the district committee on ordained ministry. Approval of the candidate must be by two-thirds written ballot and the candidate shall have been graduated from an accredited high school or received a certificate of equivalency.

2. Candidates approved by the charge conference and seeking to become certified for licensed or ordained ministry shall:

   a) request to meet with the district committee on ordained ministry. In preparation for meeting with the district committee on ordained ministry, consult with the mentor to provide the following written information, in addition to the material written for ¶311.1.d:

      i) the most formative experience of their Christian life

      ii) God's call to licensed or ordained ministry and role of the church in their call

      iii) their beliefs as a Christian

      iv) their gifts for ministry

      v) their present understanding of their call to ministry as elder, deacon, or licensed ministry; and

      vi) their support system

   b) complete and release required psychological reports, criminal background, and credit checks. They shall submit, on a form provided by the conference board of ordained ministry:

      i) a notarized statement detailing any convictions for felony or misdemeanor or written accusations of sexual misconduct or child abuse; or

      ii) a notarized statement certifying that this candidate has neither been accused in writing nor convicted of a felony, misdemeanor, any incident of sexual misconduct, or child abuse.

The district committee on ordained ministry through the board of ordained ministry shall seek ways to consider cultural and ethnic/racial realities in meeting these requirements.

   c) provide other information as the district committee may require for determining gifts, evidence of God's grace, fruit, and demonstration of the call to licensed or ordained ministry; and

   d) agree for the sake of the mission of Jesus Christ in the world and the most effective witness of the gospel, and in consideration of their influence as clergy, to make a complete dedication of themselves to the highest ideals of the Christian life as set forth in ¶¶ 102-104; 160-166. To this end they shall agree to exercise responsible self-control by personal habits conducive to bodily health, mental and emotional maturity, fidelity in marriage and celibacy in singleness, social responsibility, and growth in grace and the knowledge and love of God. Where possible, the local church is encouraged to assist candidates with the expenses of candidacy.

e) Upon vote of certification, shall be encouraged by the district committee on ordained ministry to attend a United Methodist seminary.

3. In special circumstances, the district committee on ordained ministry may authorize other United Methodist ministry settings to serve in the role of the local church for the purpose of recommending candidacy and specify the persons or bodies that will serve in the roles of pastor, pastor/staff parish relations committee and charge conference.

Candidacy Process for the Deacon, Elder, and Local Pastor

Inquiring Candidate: 2008 *Book of Discipline* ¶311

1. Contact the pastor in the local church, another deacon or elder, or the DS
2. Read The Christian as Minister (recommended, not required)
3. Participate in Ministry Inquiry Process (recommended, not required)

Beginning Candidacy: ¶311.1.*a-c* (apply & enroll)

1. Member of The United Methodist Church or baptized participant of a recognized United Methodist campus ministry or other United Methodist ministry setting for one (1) year
2. Apply to DS, in writing, for admission to candidacy program and be assigned a candidacy mentor by DS/dCOM; include statement of call
3. Complete candidacy online enrollment and $75 payment
4. Complete beginning stages of candidacy with candidacy mentor

Declaring Candidacy: ¶311.1.*d,e* (declaring)

1. Consult with pastor or equivalent in ministry setting and request recommendation from S/P-PRC or equivalent
2. High school degree or equivalent
3. Written statement of call; responses to Wesley's historic questions in ¶310; and interview by Pastor/Staff Parish Relations Committee or equivalent
4. Recommendation by charge conference or equivalent as specified by district committee
5. Continue candidacy program with candidacy mentor and academic requirements

Certified Candidate: ¶311.2

Completion of the following:
1. Written response to ministry questions in ¶311.2a as well as ¶310
2. Psychological assessment, criminal background, and credit check
3. Provide other information upon request
4. Agree to make a complete dedication of themselves to the highest ideals of the Christian life
5. Examination and approval by dCOM

Local Pastor - Completed candidacy certification, licensed, and assigned a clergy mentor ¶314

Continuing Candidacy: ¶312

1. Annual recommendation by charge conference
2. Annual interview and approval by dCOM
3. Annual report of satisfactory progress of studies and copy of transcripts from university or school of theology

Completing Candidacy: ¶324

1. Certified candidate for minimum of one (1) year, maximum twelve (12) years
2. One (1) year in service ministry
3. Completion of one-half the basic graduate theological studies to be eligible for commissioning.
4. Health certificate completed by medical doctor
5. Written and oral doctrinal exam and written autobiographical statement
6. Interview and recommendation by three-fourths vote of dCOM
7. Notarized statement certifying that the candidate has neither been accused in writing nor convicted of a felony, misdemeanor, or any incident of sexual misconduct or child abuse
8. Interview and recommendation by the BOM
9. Election to provisional membership by clergy session

Commissioning to specialized ministry as provisional member

Candidacy Check List

Your personal log sheet

Completed reading and review of *The Christian as Minister*. (Recommended but not required.)

Date completed _____ Place _____

Completed *Understanding God's Call: A Ministry Inquiry Process*. (Recommended but not required.)

Date completed _____ Place _____

Date of letter and statement of call to district superintendent _____

_____

Date of application and online enrollment into the candidacy program (Form 101) _____

Date of online signature of district superintendent on Form 101 _____

_____

District superintendent's name _____

Address _____

_____

Telephone (with Area Code) _____

E-mail _____ Fax _____

Date of online signature of candidacy mentor on application
Form 101 _____

Mentor's Name _____

Mentor Address _____

_____

Telephone (with Area Code) _____

E-mail _____ Fax _____

Date of completing online Inventory of Religious Activities and Interests (IRAI) _____

Date IRAI reviewed with candidacy mentor _____

Date of completion of psychological assessment instruments and sent to be scored _____

Date of consultation with psychological assessment specialist _____

Meeting(s) with your **local church/faith community staff committee**:

Name of committee _____

Chairperson's name _____

E-mail _____ Phone _____

Names of members of committee:

_____   _____

_____   _____

_____   _____

_____   _____

Date of recommendation by local committee: _____

Date of annual renewals by local committee:

_____   _____   _____

_____   _____   _____

Recommendation of your **charge conference or equivalent named by dCOM**:

Date of meeting _____ Place _____

Name of charge conference or equivalent _____

Presiding officer _____

Email _____

Record of vote regarding recommendation: For _____ Against _____

You may attach a copy of your written response to the candidacy questions (¶311.2a, Discipline) after this page.

Meeting with your dCOM for approval as certified candidate:

Date _____ Time _____ Place _____

Chairperson's name _____

Telephone _____ E-mail _____

Names of committee members:

_____   _____

_____   _____

_____   _____

Record of sessions with candidacy mentor:

Date and Time   Topics, Remarks, Needed preparation

_____   _____

                      _____

                      _____

_____   _____

                      _____

                      _____

_____   _____

                      _____

                      _____

_____   _____

                      _____

                      _____

_____   _____

                      _____

                      _____

_____   _____

                      _____

                      _____

_____   _____

                      _____

                      _____

_____   _____

                      _____

                      _____

Date you reviewed candidacy mentor's report in preparation for dCOM
certification interview _____

You may want to include a copy of that report here.
Use additional sheets as needed for other interviews, notes, and relevant
information.

Section 2:
Beginning Candidacy

Called to Licensed or Ordained Ministry

The purpose of this section is to explore your call from the perspective of God's grace, your gifts, and fruit in more specific ways: Through contemplation of your inner life and interaction with the spiritual disciplines; through the experience of religious inventories and psychological assessment instruments and follow-up conversations; through reflection about your relationships with others; and through discerning your fruit through service and successes and failures.

As you enter this time of contemplation, interaction, and reflection, you may begin with the following or another prayer:

> *As we focus on grace, gifts, and fruit in more specific ways, enable us to recognize how these parts relate to each other and how this study informs me about my call to ministry. Holy Spirit, you know I want to know your love and will and desire to do it. I ask for the grace of being able to recognize your presence in my life and to be aware of what you want me to do next. Amen.*

As you begin this section, identify the units and topics that are especially important for considering your calling and decisions about licensed or ordained ministry in a way that gives consideration to your background and experience.

See Appendix E (pg. 227) *Understanding God's Call: A Ministry Inquiry Process* for additional resources to explore God's call through the Bible, your experience and God's presence.

Recognizing and Experiencing Grace

In todays time the historic term examiners include your candidacy mentor, local church or other authorized United Methodist ministry setting, dCOM, your spiritual director, or others with whom you consult in your candidacy studies and exploration.

The hope is that you and all involved will experience God's grace in ways that invite honesty and offer new insight.

Grace pervades our understanding of Christian faith and life. By grace we mean the undeserved, unmerited, and loving action of God in human existence through the ever-present Holy Spirit. (¶101, Discipline)

God's free gift of unconditional acceptance and forgiveness to all is central to Christian experience in every generation and at every age. Experiencing grace fully is the foundation for becoming a faithful Christian, exploring life and claiming wholeness, living in discipleship, and reaching out to others. As a licensed or ordained clergy, you will exemplify a life of recognizing and experiencing grace to, with, and on behalf of others.

Grace and Examiners

It is significant that Wesley addressed the questions about grace, gifts, and fruit to the examiners in those early days, rather than directly to candidates for ministry. The questions as they were printed on page 18 in this book and in the *Discipline*, ¶310, are stated in such a way to ask the examiners for their observations of grace, gifts and demonstration of fruits within the candidate. Sometimes when a person is asked directly to describe or ascertain something about him or herself, it is easy to distort reality or to be blind to what others can see more clearly. When others ask out of love from an observer point of view, it may leave room for the Holy Spirit to blow fresh winds into a situation or to allow gently probing winds to open up blind spots or closed up minds and hearts.

In today's time the term examiners includes your candidacy mentor, local church, or other authorized United Methodist ministry setting, district committee on ordained ministry, your spiritual director, or others with whom you consult in your candidacy studies. It is hoped that you can trust God's grace to be prevalent in all areas of your life through these relationships.

Your candidacy mentor and the *Guidelines for Candidacy* will confront you repeatedly in many ways with questions and issues that ask you to examine how you experience God's grace in your inner life (physical, emotional, mental, intentions, etc.) and in all your relationships. In your candidacy process, the hope and prayer is that candidate, candidacy mentor, the church, and all involved will experience God's grace in ways that invite honesty and offer new insight.

Reflections to Recognize and Experience Grace

Select from below the options that seem most helpful for you:

Consider biblical discussions of grace, such as Romans 3-12 and Ephesians 2-4. Describe how grace frees a person to be in relationship with God.

Share one or two descriptions of situations in which you received grace.

Describe a time when you were especially aware of being an instrument of God's grace. You may relate the prayer of St. Francis (*The United Methodist Hymnal*, No. 481) to your experience.

Reflect on your experiences in leadership and how grace was manifested in these relationships.

Describe grace so a child can experience and understand God's grace. Refer to examples of grace and faith that Jesus valued in children (Mark 9:33-37, 10:13-16, and parallel scriptures in Matthew and Luke).

Grace Realized through Spiritual Formation

A perspective on spiritual disciplines

Practicing spiritual disciplines is a sacred matter. You may already be using variations or combinations of these disciplines. You may use your time together to describe what makes a discipline useful to you, which factors help you maintain your practices for spiritual growth, and which of these have guided you in your discernment.

See Appendix E (pg. 227) *Understanding God's Call: A Ministry Inquiry Process* for additional reflection and resources for spiritual formation.

Spiritual disciplines are means of grace to open yourself to God's presence and leading. You may already experience them as a way of living and growing. For spiritual disciplines to be effective as means of grace, they need to be incorporated into daily and weekly patterns. They can offer a grace-full way of living.

Christians across the generations have found God's grace through six classical disciplines. You are invited to practice them in any order in which you feel led. You may even want to adopt one or more as permanent disciplines. Take your time so you can become inwardly quiet enough to listen for and hear the Spirit's word to you.

As you explore each of these ways by which God can reach into the depths of your being and shape your spirit, trust God's presence and call to you. Allow your energy to be centered on the Holy Spirit and its leading for you.

Practicing Spiritual Disciplines

1. Devotional Bible study

Praying the scripture means you sit before a text and listen for what God is saying to you, individually or corporately, through that text.

When you read scripture in a prayerful way, you are not trying to memorize it or figure out what to say about it, or even garner its truth. The attitude you bring is open and expectant. Read each word slowly, and if one word or phrase causes a reaction inside of you, stop and linger on that word or phrase. The reaction inside you may feel pleasant or unpleasant. Whatever it is, you stay with it for as long as it is speaking to you. Let your imagination bring you into the scene and fill your senses.

Read John 1:35-51 and its parallels (Matthew 4:18-22; Mark 1:16-20; Luke 5:2-11). Ask God to give you the grace of being aware of God's presence as you read. Now read the verses slowly. Read them again if you wish. Now, close your eyes and imagine that you are present in the story with Jesus. When you have completed your meditation, respond to the following questions:

Bible Study Questions:

a. When Jesus passed by you, what were you talking about?

b. Were you led to follow him? Did you? What were you feeling?

c. If you followed him to where he was staying, where was it? Who or what else was there?

d. Did you want to stay there? Did you want to stay with the others?

e. Do you sense in these passages a message about you and licensed or ordained ministry?

2. Journaling

If you wrote your responses to the questions above as you listened to the scripture, you were journaling. Journaling is writing about what is going on inside of you. It assumes that God is present not only in other people, events, and writings, but certainly within you. So journaling is a way of hearing God's voice within you.

You can write about anything—especially what you are thinking, feeling, experiencing, and those experiences and relationships for which you are hungering, afraid, or grateful. Journaling is similar to a diary, but a diary is like a map of known territory, while a journal moves you beyond the known to encounter the less explored terrain of your spirit.

You may want to keep a separate book of some kind for your continuing journal entries to honor your own journey. Because of the personal nature of a journal, you will probably want to take care to keep others from reading it. Since these written words are between you and God, you will probably be free enough to express yourself to God only if you are sure no one else will read what you write. If you live with other people, negotiate this privacy with them.

Suggestions for your journal—begin with the ones that attract you.

a. Memories of being baptized (based on stories told to me or my own memory).

b. My responses to Luke 24:13-35 – The Walk to Emmaus

c. When I first heard God's call to be a licensed or ordained minister.

d. Two people who have influenced my life in faith, and how they have influenced me.

e. An event when I saw Jesus working in others and how it affected me.

f. My doubts about becoming a licensed or ordained minister.

g. My hopes and dreams for licensed or ordained ministry.

h. Think of one experience in the last week and ask how God might be speaking to you through that experience, especially as it relates to your consideration of licensed or ordained ministry. Record your reflections in your journal.

3. Private prayer

Prayer is the essence of all the activities of spiritual formation, because prayer is the act of being in touch with God. In the usual way of praying, words are involved. You praise God, you ask God for forgiveness, you ask for God's activity in your life or others, and you offer gratitude.

Prayer is awe inspiring (or mysterious) because somehow, when you speak, God hears, and somehow when God speaks, you hear. You cannot explain how it happens. God, human beings, and creation, communicate. Sometimes prayer is simply being with God, without and beyond words, just being present to each other.

When you listen to scripture or journal, you pray. When you speak to a friend about your spirit or theirs, you pray. When you read about others' thoughts and experiences of God, you pray. When you are silent and alone before God, you pray.

You may use a visual symbol for God, such as a cross, lighted candle, a picture of Jesus or other meaningful reminder of God's presence. The symbol may be something in your home, workplace, or on your person like a cross on a ring or necklace or in your pocket or wallet. You may use music or other art forms that help you to focus on and be open to God's presence in your life.

Anne Morrow Lindbergh suggested that sometimes the place of solitude is in the midst of the busy daily work, such as the drive to your work setting in early morning traffic; enjoying God's creation out the kitchen window while doing dishes; or openness to God's presence as you work in your garden.

In whatever time you choose, simply be there. These thoughts may open your awareness to God's presence:
- a period during which God healed you
- God is love and loves me
- how good it feels to be at home
- a deep, persistent need
- a constant hope
- favorite words of scripture repeated over and over

4. Spiritual reading

Spiritual reading can open your mind and heart to God and is another way to pray. Often people hear God while they are reading the Bible, a collection of sermons, a book of prayers, a novel, news of current events, personal accounts of faith, and more.

There is an annotated bibliography at the end of this guidebook that offers many suggested readings in spirituality. These resources provide helpful information about how to make yourself available to the Spirit so you can be formed or guided. They also, at the very moment you are reading them, can put you in touch with God.

Spiritual reading is followed by questions for reflection. For example, read John 13:5-8 and then reflect on the following paragraph by Flora Slosson Wuellner in *Prayer and Our Bodies* (Upper Room Books, 1987, p. 38). The questions are intended to evoke, rather than limit, your reflection.

> *"Peter certainly felt that [he wanted to be a giver rather than the receiver] at the last supper in the upper room, when Jesus knelt before him to wash his feet (John 13:5-8). Peter was startled and protesting. Any one of us would probably have felt the same. But Jesus told him both firmly and lovingly that learning to receive is as much a part of belonging as learning to give."*

Questions from spiritual reading (John 13:5-8):

a. What of God's nature does this description show you?

b. What might Wuellner be saying to you about how God is calling you?

c. What do you want to give? How easy is this for you?

d. What do you want to receive? How easy is this for you?

e. What do you need? How do you feel about asking for it?

5. Spiritual guide

Another way God can guide you along your spirit's way is through a spiritual friend. Other names for this person may be soul friend, spiritual director, or spiritual mentor.

Spiritual mentoring is based on the assumption that the Holy Spirit is always the source of guidance and is a relationship that is more intense, more personal, and more open than most other relationships. Your spiritual director should be someone other than your candidacy mentor. That will keep the two types of relationships clear for you.

A spiritual mentor is a man or woman whom you select and who covenants with you to listen to you speak about your relationship with God in Jesus Christ. The role of your spiritual mentor or spiritual friend is to listen with you to what the Holy Spirit may be speaking to you, to speak as led by God, to accept you where you are, to encourage you to look ever more closely for God's presence in every-day life, and at times, to suggest steps that might help you grow.

Useful feedback from spiritual mentors can add new perspectives to corporate worship, the institutional church, or small groups within it, as well as to your own prayer life.

Questions to reflect with your mentor or spiritual guide:

a. What part of my call to licensed or ordained ministry is coming from within myself and what part is coming from others?

b. What am I hearing during prayer time about my call?

c. How is scripture guiding or not guiding me about my call?

d. What are things I am seeing about myself as I journal, especially ways I am growing and changing?

e. What doubts, fears, conflicts, and changes do I recognize in my life? Where is God in these?

6. Silence and stillness for meditation

Silence sets you free from having to speak: liberating you from superfluous and artificial speaking that is a way to avoid God, yourself, and others; or a way to make an impression on someone (1 Corinthians 13). Silence can clear your mind and unclog your entry portals. The spiritual discipline of silence is stopping all the voices in your mind so you hear the still, small voice of God with greater clarity and depth.

If stillness and retreat times seem empty and scary, trace the sources of these fears. Unmasking fears can free you to be more open to experience God's presence and guidance.

Seek to replace your fears with confidence that God comes to you in silence and still small voices (1 Kings 19:1-18; Mark 4:35-41). As you put distractions aside, you can reawaken to God's presence and the unlimited, expansive nature of God's love. As you empty yourself of speech, you can become full of love, expectation and openness to God. Silence has power.

The wonderful paradox is that as soon as you are set free by silence and solitude, the Jesus whom you meet there sends you back again to speech and community. Jesus has no desire for you to withdraw permanently from others. When you are guided by the Holy Spirit, then your life of prayer and your life of service are inseparable. Each nourishes the other into life for all creation.

One of the best ways to look for silence is to take a personal retreat for a period of silence longer than your daily prayer time. Twenty-four hours may be a useful length of time. Radios, televisions, and books are not needed. Your Bible, a prayer guide, and a journal are sufficient.

You are invited to try a personal spiritual retreat. If you are already accustomed to this type of renewal, go again during your decision-making time. When you arrive at your destination, ask Jesus for the grace you need. Do you need rest? Do you need to get clear about your own skills? Do you need courage? Do you need patience? What do you need?

Put yourself in God's care; ask for what you need; listen and pray for guidance to respond.

From Grace to Gifts: A Transition

Remember that gifts are given you by God and are the talents, abilities, and skills you bring to licensed or ordained ministry and your promise for leadership. Gifts are always considered in relationship. Through grace we recognize our abilities and skills and evaluate their usefulness in relationship to both current and future ministries. Through grace we recognize and accept both the gifts and limitations that we have. When we know that God loves us consistently and unconditionally, we are free to explore any aspect of life with openness and honesty.

The second set of Wesley's questions to examiners concentrates on gifts (¶310, *Discipline*): "Have they [the candidates] a clear, sound understanding; a right judgment in the things of God; a just conception of salvation by faith? Do they speak justly, readily, clearly?"

With your candidacy mentor, review your reflections on naming and assessing your gifts that you did in *A Ministry Inquiry Process* if you used it.

With your candidacy mentor consider your gifts now and how they can be used in licensed or ordained ministry.

The Gift of IRAI Results

This section assumes that you and your candidacy mentor have received your IRAI results. If you have not, first complete the IRAI and have your results in hand to benefit from this material.

The IRAI is neither a test to be passed nor a secret way to determine whether you should or should not enter licensed or ordained ministry.

The next four chapters offer guidelines to look at and define your gifts for ministry. The formal candidacy process begins with an inventory of your own interests, talents, skills, and values, and how these fit the requirements for licensed or ordained ministry (the IRAI). You have already done this in many ways. Yet these next chapters help you acknowledge and assess your gifts in more systematic ways:

- Using the IRAI results
- Using results from psychological assessment
- Using information from family and others for self-understanding

The Inventory of Religious Activities and Interests

The Inventory of Religious Activities and Interests (IRAI) helps you obtain a more accurate overview of your interests, goals, experiences, motivations, and personality. Seeing these together gives you a resource for discussing your vocational vision and for evaluating how your interests, abilities, and potential fit licensed or ordained ministry.

The IRAI is neither a test to be passed nor a secret way to determine whether you should or should not enter licensed or ordained ministry. The inventory profile clusters questions together to give you information about the types of church-related work that you enjoy and other activities that you find less interesting.

By looking at personal, family, and other background factors, you can consider motivations for your interest in the various types of ministry. Use these sections to review your IRAI results. You are encouraged to add notes for discussion with your candidacy mentor.

Your personal background

The first 39 questions of the IRAI survey your educational, religious, and interpersonal background. These questions also ask you to describe yourself and your family and indicate some of your goals, objectives, and abilities.

Most of these questions can be used in conversation with your candidacy mentor as guides to exploring your interests and your evaluation of the influence of relatives and friends on you.

Although your answers are important, even more vital is your reflection on the answers as a way of gaining self understanding. You may also want to use these questions in your discussions with your spouse, a close friend, or with relatives.

Ministry interests

A large set of questions enables you to match your interests to the types of activities that are often done by persons in church-related work settings.

Licensed and ordained ministers perform many types of services and activities. Among these, each will have a unique pattern of interests, preferences, and priorities, and emphases for the church. The IRAI scales combine interests into more general themes that identify these patterns.

IRAI scales are measures of your interests. Interests are often related to abilities since it is more likely that you will be interested in doing those things that you can do well. It is also possible to have interests in which you have less ability.

The results of the IRAI may allow you to identify interests for which you can plan to obtain needed training in seminary, special courses, or workshops. Practice with supervision also enables you to become proficient in areas of interest.

Values and goals

The IRAI also asks you to rank your values and goals as a way to examine your motivations for licensed or ordained ministry.

Add other values and goals that did not appear in the IRAI listing.

How do your goals, ideals, values, standards, and expectations match those of licensed or ordained ministry?

Which of your values may be in conflict with the standards usually expected of licensed or ordained ministers?

Self-rated abilities

In the IRAI you rated skills that are often needed by licensed and ordained ministers.

Add other skills that you think are needed by licensed and ordained ministers; then rate yourself on them.

How much of each of these abilities do you have? To what extent can you learn these skills? How?

The priorities you give to your skills and interests are expressions of your values. You may have interest and/or skill in an area yet consider it less, or more, important than other interests or abilities.

Your priority listing of the 10 IRAI ministry interest scales measures the value you give to each area.

Review your priorities and add your estimate of how well you do, and can learn to do, each of these types of ministry. You may mark these on your IRAI profile.

Interests, abilities, motivation, and action

Becoming competent and effective in licensed or ordained ministry results when your interests, talents, abilities, and motivations blend to produce consistent patterns of constructive actions.

You may have much interest in an area but lack the talent or ability to do well in that area. You may even have both interest and ability, yet not value the area as important for licensed or ordained ministry. Thus, you may not be motivated to develop your potential in this area.

Describe three or four areas where your interests, talents, abilities, and motivations support your call to licensed or ordained ministry. How do you feel about these?

Identify places where your gifts, or lack of gifts, do not seem to support your call to licensed or ordained ministry. In what ways might these areas become stress points or conflicts for you as you consider entering licensed or ordained ministry?

Where your interests, talents, values, and motivations do not seem to support your call to licensed or ordained ministry; do these differences raise questions about your call? How does this information help you discern your gifts and your call to licensed or ordained ministry?

Evaluation by others

You will gain much from the candid feedback about your promise for effectiveness in licensed or ordained ministry from others who know you well and have observed you in action in your local church, work, or other settings.

You may want to get feedback from a friend or family member as to your strengths and weaknesses for licensed or ordained ministry. How do their answers compare with your IRAI results?

Feedback from others helps you calibrate your own judgments about how your values and skills produce results (fruit, or evidences of the Spirit).

Review your IRAI results with your candidacy mentor. Try to check on the accuracy of your own evaluations of your interests, skills, values, motivations, and standards for effectiveness in licensed or ordained ministry so that you can discern how the Holy Spirit is leading you now.

The Gift of Psychological Assessment

Psychological assessment is a contemporary method for doing the deep soul-searching that is modeled in the scriptures and is one of several ways you and the church examine your fitness and potential for effectiveness in licensed or ordained ministry in relation to your calling.

As you enter this time of reflection, we encourage you to review one or more of the scriptures below that describe the depth and breadth of God's searching one's being so that a person can bear good fruit in active service: Psalms 139; John 15; 1 Corinthians 12-14; Romans 12-15.

A perspective on Psychological Assessment

You have answered several inventories and given much personal information about yourself. If you think this is too personal or intrusive, consider the process from this larger perspective.

Assessment of personality factors using personal information is essential in most careers. For example, when an airline entrusts the lives of hundreds of passengers and a multimillion dollar aircraft to a pilot, the airline has a right to know details of that pilot's life that contribute to the safety of the flights he or she operates.

The United Methodist Church entrusts the lives of hundreds of parishioners and parish resources to the care and guidance of its deacons, elders, and local pastors.

In psychological assessment there are two clients. Both are equally important.

- You, as a candidate, are the client with the need to know your own functioning in relation to your calling.
- The church is also the client with the need to know whether to entrust you with licensed or ordained ministry.

When done properly by a qualified professional who also knows the needs of the church and its licensed or ordained ministry, psychological assessment can be a helpful source of information to consider as you discern your Christian calling.

An Opportunity and a Caution

Psychological assessment can suggest some areas that you might explore further. You can often see relationships between your

The GBHEM Division of Ordained Ministry has recommended to annual conference boards of ordained ministry a standard procedure for psychological assessment of candidates.

If your annual conference uses a procedure that is different from the DOM recommendations the **candidacy mentor** should understand and guide the candidate in the appropriate process required by his or her BOM.

It is assumed that you have already completed our psychological assessment with a ministry assessment specialist (MAS) and received feedback from this report.

The *Book of Discipline* requires that you complete your psychological assessment prior to being approved as a certified candidate.

Your **candidacy mentor** can give your details of the procedure for your annual conference.

You may choose to share and discuss your psychological report with your candidacy mentor (but it is not required) as you explore implications of your psychological assessment for licensed or ordained ministry.

thoughts, feelings, motivations, values, goals, and actions that you might otherwise overlook.

There is nothing magic or super accurate about a psychological inventory or about a computer-generated inventory profile. These are not direct messages from God or anyone else about what you should or should not be.

Assessment information is of no greater or lesser importance than the other sources discussed in these candidacy studies. It should neither be ignored nor given too much importance.

The Fit Between You and Licensed or Ordained Ministry

There are complex relationships between your personality and the kinds of settings in which you work best. Because of the tasks that clergy do, personal characteristics that you might otherwise ignore may become more important if you enter the licensed or ordained ministry as a Christian vocation, and if you serve in certain types of ministry settings.

A person may be psychologically healthy and mature, yet lack the motivations and personality characteristics that are needed by licensed or ordained ministers. Psychological assessment is designed to help you clarify your personality strengths and weaknesses in relation to the requirements for licensed or ordained ministry.

Psychological assessment and consultation may identify potential difficulties for you if you enter licensed or ordained ministry. Growth counseling or therapy may be beneficial to you before you make long-range decisions about vocational choices. Personal, marriage, or group therapy may offer other ways for you to change that will benefit both you, those who are close to you, and those whom you may serve in the future.

Basic Elements in the Psychological Assessment Process

Once you have completed your assessment, the following four guides can assist you to use this process more effectively in discerning your call and future directions.

1. Personal Background Factors

The personal data you provide in the Personal Data Inventory (PDI) as part of the candidacy online enrollment system, as well as part of the IRAI and the autobiographical information you complete online, enable you to consider the influence of family, work, and other experiences on your calling and future effectiveness for licensed or ordained ministry. You can also connect this information to the heritage sessions of the Ministry Inquiry Process if you used that process.

List some background factors you want to explore further:

Your candidacy mentor may help you understand the process and the purpose of the psychological assessment, using the guides listed here.

It is your choice whether or not you decide to share the results of the psychological assessment from the ministerial assessment specialist.

2. References from Persons who Know You Well

Persons who provide information about you as part of the psychological assessment procedure are asked to provide confidential and candid comments about the patterns, strengths, and growth areas they see in you. These careful observations contribute to the validity, reliability, and usefulness of your psychological assessment.

The value of statements from references grows out of the fact that they come from persons who have experienced you in a variety of situations, including times when you may not have been at your best. The reports from references are confidential in an effort to encourage them to be honest and frank without harming your relationship.

Which persons who know you well can give you caring and careful feedback about your future effectiveness in licensed or ordained ministry?

What enables you to be open to this feedback? What helps them to be honest with you, as well as the church?

3. Personality Measures

The scoring of the assessment instruments used either through the service of the General Board of Higher Education and Ministry or through the services of your annual conference uses patterns of answers to arrive at summary statements about your potentials and tendencies.

Among personality characteristics that affect your promise for effective licensed or ordained ministry are the following:

- cognitive clarity vs. being confused, biased, rigid, or judgmental in handling information
- good ego-strength, emotional stability, and empathy vs. insensitivity, excessive mood swings, depression, or anxiety
- comfort in being with others, independence, and cooperation vs. attempts to dominate, withdraw, or overly depend on others
- comfortable and flexible self-control vs. being impulsive, immature, antisocial, defensive, inhibited, or passive-aggressive
- appropriate respect for and cooperation with those in authority over you vs. conflicts with those in authority or ignoring rules and procedures
- a healthy sense of nurture and support from others vs. feelings of loneliness and lack of support from others, conflicts with family, sexual conflicts
- regular habits of health and personal care, exercise, eating, and weight control vs. abuse of your body, expressing emotions through physical symptoms, or abusive use of food, drugs, or beverages.

Which personality issues were revealed that you need to explore further?

What are your strengths and areas of needed growth?

What plans can you develop to address these areas as you prepare for licensed or ordained ministry?

4. Recommendations

The suggestions and recommendations from your ministerial assessment specialist invite you to consider how the information from your psychological assessment can help you discern your call, identify issues that need your attention, and plan ways to increase your effectiveness in licensed or ordained ministry.

Suggestions for supervision, personal and/or other therapy, additional study, and other next steps are in the final section of the ministerial assessment specialist's report.

Consider these recommendations carefully so that you can arrive at a plan of action for addressing any concerns or contingencies that may be in the ministerial assessment specialist's report. These are hypotheses or hunches to guide you in your next steps concerning the psychological aspects of your calling.

The dCOM may discuss some of these recommendations and decide to assign certain next steps to complete before you can be approved as a candidate for licensed or ordained ministry.

What implications do these recommendations have for your fitness for licensed or ordained ministry?

A physical examination checks symptoms as a basis for identifying causes and prescribing treatment. Likewise, psychological assessment seeks to identify basic personality dimensions and suggest types of growth in order to be of maximum effectiveness and service in licensed or ordained ministry. This growth may also occur in other ways that are suggested in this guidebook.

In this space make notes about your plan of action for implementing specific recommendations:

The Gift of Family Relationships

Your Family Relationships

You are *like* everyone else. You were born of a mother and father, and set among caregivers in a particular family structure. You learned a native language, you grew and developed family characteristics, and you have been affected by the many changes to family and world structures of the 20th century.

You are *unique*. No one else, even an identical twin, is exactly like you in every detail. You have your own identity and your own characteristics.

As an adult, you have taken control of your own life and assumed the responsibilities and privileges of being a citizen of this world. You have created your own household, and your own family situation.

Diagram or describe your current family structure and relationships.

How have your family experiences influenced how you plan to serve in ministry?

Choose to explore the situations and issues in this chapter that fit your circumstance, or adapt the questions to fit your circumstance.

The candidacy mentor is encouraged to be flexible and adjust the procedures and conversations to enable you to obtain maximum benefit.

What new insights have come to you about the influence of your current family and your family of origin in your decision to follow a call to licensed or ordained ministry?

Which family of origin issues do you need to continue to address so that you can be more effective in living out your calling?

How might your career decisions affect those closest to you? How can you be proactive in communicating and preparing those around you for those decisions?

Your Current Lifestyle

The following groups of comments and questions relate to all family lifestyles, whether you are single, married, or in a long-term relationship. Select and modify the ones that fit your own situation as you explore these issues.

Your family status and lifestyle do not indicate how effective you will be in licensed or ordained ministry; yet your family status and relationships have many complex associations with your possible career as a licensed or ordained minister.

Single Lifestyle

If you are single and have never been married, or are divorced and not remarried, consider that the reasons leading up to and the circumstances of either may affect how you practice licensed or ordained ministry in subtle ways. Among these may be committing to a ministry that does not allow time for family relationships; being appointed to a place where it may not be easy to find or attract a partner; anger or hurt about marriage and family experiences; lack of interest in marriage; sexual identity issues; or underlying emotional conditions, such as anger at the other gender or your previous partner.

The traditional assumption about United Methodist licensed or ordained ministers is that they are, or soon will be, married. Although this assumption is changing toward acceptance of other lifestyles for licensed or ordained clergy persons, you may experience a bias that others (especially in the appointments where you serve) would like you to be married.

If you plan to remain single, how will you explain your decision to parishioners, colleagues, and others who may prefer that their licensed or ordained minister(s) be married? How will you cope positively with those who may try to find you a marriage partner, date you, or question your choices? How will you react if you find that you are attracted to someone in the appointment where you are serving?

If you plan to marry, reflect how your new status may affect those to whom you minister and how the change will also impact your lifestyle and ministry.

If you are now in a relationship that may lead to marriage, involve your partner in discussions about how your possible marriage and your potential spouse's future career or vocation relate to your future Christian vocation and faith issues. How will you commit to itinerancy (as an elder) or accepting another appointment (as a deacon) that takes into consideration the needs and expectations of you and your spouse?

Every person entering licensed or ordained ministry needs a support structure for times of difficulty, conflict, failure, success, and transition.

As a single person, to whom will you turn for the ongoing support you need? What are your dependable support groups? What relatives and friends give you support and encouragement in pursuing licensed or ordained ministry?

As a single licensed or ordained minister, marriage-like arrangements such as unmarried couples living together are not acceptable. Consider your own expressions of sexuality in relation to these standards set by the *Book of Discipline*.

> *¶304.2 For the sake of the mission of Jesus Christ in the world and the most effective witness to the Christian gospel, and in consideration of the influence of an ordained minister on the lives of other persons both within and outside the Church, the Church expects those who seek ordination to make a complete dedication of themselves to the highest ideals of the Christian life. To this end, they agree to exercise responsible self-control by personal habits conducive to bodily health, mental and emotional maturity, integrity in all personal relationships, fidelity in marriage and celibacy in singleness, social responsibility, and growth in grace and in the knowledge and love of God.*

> *¶304.3 While persons set apart by the Church for ordained ministry are subject to all the frailties of the human condition and the pressures of society, they are required to maintain the highest standards of holy living in the world. Since the practice of homosexuality is incompatible with Christian teaching, self-avowed practicing homosexuals are not to be accepted as candidates, ordained as ministers, or appointed to serve in The United Methodist Church.*

Note questions for discussion with your candidacy mentor here.

Married Lifestyle

If you are married, take this opportunity to invite your spouse into your vocational discussions if you have not already done so.

As a married person to whom will you turn for ongoing support? What are your dependable support groups?

As a married person, how will you build a healthy support system beyond your marriage? While your spouse will often be the one who gives you the most support, it is important to have others you can turn to as well.

If you choose to enter licensed or ordained ministry, your marriage will go through a period of adjustment; perhaps a period of stress and change.

What resources are available to support your marriage through this period of transition?

What issues may be important for you and your spouse as you consider a vocation in licensed or ordained ministry?

How does your spouse feel about the possibility of becoming a licensed or ordained minister's spouse?

How do you and your spouse feel about the church's concern and support for your marriage in relation to your future licensed or ordained ministry?

How is your consideration of a vocation in licensed or ordained ministry impacted by your spouse's career?

How will you commit to honor itinerancy (as an elder) or accepting another appointment (as a deacon) and also take into consideration the needs and expectations of you and your spouse?

Divorced, Widowed, and Single-Parent Lifestyles

Although a traditional, married lifestyle is most common among licensed or ordained ministers, some ministers live in other family situations. If you are in one of these, you need to explore how your lifestyle will relate to a possible vocation in licensed or ordained ministry.

Divorced and not remarried

What have you learned about yourself as a result of your divorce that may have an impact on your ministry decision?

Widowed

If you have experienced the death of your spouse, how have you responded to the loss, to subsequent experiences of bereavement, and to being a widow or widower? How may this affect your work in licensed or ordained ministry?

In the context of your Christian faith, how has your understanding of death and life been enriched or changed as a result of your experience?

Single parent issues

If you have children and are living as a one-parent family, how will this affect your possible work as a licensed or ordained minister?

What child care arrangements will you need to make to enable you to maintain the schedule of a licensed or ordained minister which often involves evenings and weekends, and occasional middle-of-the-night calls to the hospital or other emergencies?

Remarried after divorce

In what ways does it matter whether your divorce and remarriage happened recently with the knowledge of others in your church, or happened several years ago and no current friends or associates know about it now?

If you are now remarried after a previous divorce, how might this affect your effectiveness in licensed or ordained ministry? Are there child custody, visitation, child support, or other stepfamily issues that could affect your preparation for licensed or ordained ministry?

These explorations between family and a vocation in licensed or ordained ministry suggest some common issues. Describe the specific combination of issues that are most important to you as you explore and discern your calling. Discuss these issues with family members and with your candidacy mentor in ways that are most helpful to you.

The Gift of Others for Self-Understanding

Obtaining Feedback

The most helpful persons for giving you feedback are those who are able to discern effective from ineffective ministries. They must be candid and frank enough to tell the truth in their observations and be able to "speak the truth in love" (Ephesians 4:15).

While you need positive encouragement, you also need supportive critiques of your fitness from persons who have actually seen you (not just heard about you from others) doing ministries in your church and community. This is a major reason that candidates are required to serve in leadership roles in ministry settings.

There are two primary kinds of information about your abilities— objective and subjective.

- **Objective data.** One source of information consists of the objective results, the "fruit," of your activities. Some examples may be grades in school, promotion at work, or the outcome of an election for a leadership position, or other results that can be seen by any person.

- **Subjective data.** The second information source consists of the personal, subjective reports from others who know you well and have observed your work in specific situations. Those are not so much recommendations as they are candid and honest evaluations or impressions concerning your strengths and weaknesses. This second type of information may be more difficult to get because others may be less candid with you, lest they hurt your feelings, discourage you, or lose your friendship.

Having many abilities and great skills does not necessarily guarantee success in licensed or ordained ministry. Additional factors, such as your commitment to God, your interests, determination, emotional maturity, energy, hard work, willingness to learn, and the opportunities that you have, also play important roles in your success.

Sometimes it is through your reactions to your weaknesses, needed growth areas, disappointments, or lack of skill that God can work most effectively (see Hebrews 12:1-3; 2 Timothy 1:7).

Talk with your candidacy mentor about ways to obtain both accurate and supportive information about your abilities and performance. It is important also to have a variety of perspectives from several sources.

Adapt the following questions in different areas to your own situation so you can obtain as much information as possible about your gifts, grace, fruit, and future effectiveness as a licensed or ordained minister.

1. Academic and Educational Potential

Academic ability is a combination of innate ability and its application to real life situations. Having accurate evaluation of your academic skills can help you clarify how to improve them.

Results of your academic work

What grade level are you maintaining in your theological studies? If you have been out of school for some years, have you taken courses in recent years or had performance evaluations in recent training for your current occupation? Try to analyze the reasons for your academic performance.

What scores have you obtained on standardized tests of academic achievement or aptitude? You may have scores or other results from national tests such as the Scholastic Aptitude Test (SAT or College Board), the American College Test (ACT), Graduate Record Examination (GRE) or other similar measures. What was your rank or standing compared to others? Are your scores better on verbal, mathematical, or other types of abilities? What might these scores mean in relation to licensed or ordained ministry?

Reflection with your candidacy mentor
Do you believe you have the intellectual ability and motivation to prepare academically for licensed or ordained ministry? List any concern you may have about your past or future academic achievement.

2. Leadership Skills and Potential

A person may relate well with others in a group yet not be effective as a leader. Sometimes the task orientation of a leader may, for example, conflict with the group-relationship orientation of other members of the group. A good leader is able to help persons work together in order to accomplish important goals.

Evidences of your leadership accomplishments
In which groups have you been elected to office or to other leadership positions? What accomplishments occurred as a result of your leadership?

What experiences have you had in leading persons your own age? Leading persons younger than you? Leading persons older than you? In which were you more successful? Why?

Invite a friend who has observed you in a leadership role to comment honestly on your work as a leader.

How do you respond to genuine complements on your leadership? What comment about your leadership has been most difficult for you to deal with? How are persons edified by your leadership and service?

Reflection with your candidacy mentor
What do you perceive to be your strengths and weaknesses as a leader? What leadership skills do you wish to improve?

3. Interpersonal skills

Having good interpersonal skills means you are able to relate well to superiors such as managers and persons in authority; you can also elicit cooperation and good performance from those whom you lead, as well as your peers such as friends, associates, and relatives.

Constructive involvement with others also means that you can work well with a wide variety of persons without being dominated by your own feelings of hostility, rejection, or competition. This involves rapport, sensitivity, tact, and personal confidence without arrogance in social relationships. The key question is, "How well do you get along with others?"

What are your skills for working with others to accomplish important goals and enabling a group to work well together?

What types of social groups do you enjoy? What do you do for fun? What is your typical relationship to others in group situations?

Do others tend to seek you out to discuss their problems and concerns? When does this happen? How do you feel about it?

Think of a situation in which you have worked with others, such as in your local church, at school, at work, or in community organizations. What comments have your associates given to you about your work and your relationships with others in the group? How did you react to their comments and suggestions? How did you feel about having your work evaluated by others?

Reflection with your candidacy mentor

Your interpersonal skills are always changing. Any lack of skill you may discover can be an opportunity for further growth. What interpersonal skills do you feel good about? What would you like to change?

4. Participation in the Christian Community

Your intellectual aptitude, interpersonal skills, and leadership abilities are interwoven with your participation in Christian groups, as well as in your participation in other activities in community, work, school, and other settings.

Evidences of success in your local church

How long have you participated in your local church or in other United Methodist congregations? In congregations of other denominations?

What leadership roles have you had in local churches? Were these elected, assumed, or delegated? Even when you are not an official leader, do others seek your help and follow your suggestions? When? For how long?

To what extent do you support your local church financially? What percentage of your income do you contribute to your local church, to other church projects and causes beyond your local church, and to non-church charities? Do you tithe? What does tithing mean to you? Do you pay your financial commitments regularly?

What involvement have you had in activities beyond your local church, such as summer camps, district committees and workshops, leadership training opportunities, annual conference organizations, and jurisdictional, national, or international church groups?

Views of others in your local church

Identify two or three persons in your local church whom you respect and trust. With each person, describe your possible vocational interests in relation to licensed or ordained ministry. Then ask how does each person think you would respond to some common local church or other ministry situations in which you might lead, such as attending committee meetings, witnessing to persons about Christ and the church, and taking initiative to resolve conflict or achieve social reform.

5. Impact on Others

This ability is related to leadership and interpersonal skills, yet it is so important that it deserves a separate set of guiding questions. The impact that you have on others may be difficult to discuss because it involves many personal and private feelings and your sense of self-esteem.

Impact on others means the affect of your appearance, facial expressions, energy levels, speech, mannerisms, and other observable characteristics.

Asking yourself the following questions may be difficult and threatening, yet they can help you to consider your important impact on others as part of the gifts that you bring to ministry. These suggestions with your feedback are also an important way to prepare yourself to meet with the district committee and board of ordained ministry at the candidacy level and the probationary levels.

Evidences of your positive impact on others

Natural appearance: Interpersonal attractiveness is not exclusively a matter of appearance yet the licensed or ordained minister's appearance often can either open opportunites to serve or close off others from further contact.

In privacy, look at yourself in a full-length mirror. Do you appear to be confident, friendly, and warm?

Although you may feel these and other positive qualities within yourself, does your appearance express these qualities in ways that others can easily see?

Do your posture and facial expressions indicate that you are comfortable and at ease?

Does your appearance conform to good health habits?

Do you communicate an ability to cope successfully with any physical limitations?

Voice: Audiotape or videotape yourself as you are speaking to another person or to a group. Then observe yourself and listen to your vocal characteristics.

What do your voice tone, pitch, and volume say about you? Is it lively and stimulating to others?

Which vocal characteristics can you change as a result of becoming aware of them?

Mannerisms: If you have a videotape of yourself, turn off the sound and watch your body language as you talk. What does it suggest to you?

Do you notice mannerisms that seem to get in the way of your communication?

Do you have some gestures that enable more effective communication than others?

Challenging physical conditions: Disabilities are not to be construed as unfavorable health factors when a person is capable of meeting the professional standards and is physically able to render effective service as a licensed or ordained minister (¶324.8, *Discipline*). A disability does not automatically bar a person from licensed or ordained ministry.

If you have a physical challenge (or disability), what strengths have you acquired as a result of coping with this challenge?

In what ways do you anticipate this condition will affect your work as a licensed or ordained minister?

What special skills have you developed in managing your physical limitation that enable you to be effective in working with others?

Reflection with your Candidacy Mentor:

What inferences are others likely to make about you and the Christ whom you represent on the basis of your speech patterns and habits?

In what ways have your interviews in the local church regarding your leadership confirmed or undermined your sense of calling to licensed or ordained ministry? Do you have any concerns about the way you function in a local church?

What discrepancies exist between how you evaluate yourself and how you are evaluated by others? How do you account for these differences?

Ages and Stages in Life and Gender Identity–Gifts to the Church

Age-related Issues

Chronological age is not in itself an indicator of the potential for effectiveness in licensed or ordained ministry, yet age may indicate that one has had certain types of maturing experiences, opportunities for growth, or the chance to work in another career field.

There is no minimum age for obtaining certification as a candidate for licensed or ordained ministry, although the requirement of high school graduation (¶¶311, 324, *Discipline*) implies that a person usually will be at least 17 or 18 years old. Requirements for college education further imply that a person will usually be at least 21 years of age at entry to a theological school.

If you are in your teens or early 20s, consider how an educational path from high school directly into college and then seminary will effect your vocational decisions. You may have gained some work experience and insights through summer or part-time work, or through volunteer work.

In what ways have you explored careers in areas other than licensed or ordained ministry so that you have a realistic basis for comparison of work and choice in response to God's call to you?

What are your greatest concerns as a young person as you anticipate a vocation in licensed or ordained ministry in The United Methodist Church?

Discuss with your mentor if you did not enter licensed or ordained ministry, what other vocational options would you consider as your response to God's calling?

If you are in your mid-20s through 30s, you may have already experienced some measure of independence and authority. Decisions about a change in career or a call to ordained ministry may mean major changes in your marriage, your relationships, and lifestyle. It is important that you include your spouse (if married) and other relatives as appropriate in your decision process.

What are the greatest issues you foresee that may impact your family and other significant relationships as you anticipate a vocation in licensed or ordained ministry?

If you are age 40 or older, the above considerations continue to be relevant. Also, you have a choice of how you will complete your educational preparation for licensed or ordained ministry. You may complete a seminary degree, an optional route for deacon in full connection (35 years or older), or the Course of Study for licensing and/or ordination. (40 years or older).

Those over 40 who enter licensed or ordained ministry are more likely to be leaving a previous career. What are your greatest concerns at your age as you anticipate a vocation in licensed or ordained ministry? What will give up as you leave another career? What will you gain as you follow this new calling?

How much additional college and/or graduate education will you need? Is this a realistic possibility for you to complete in a reasonable time?

What family responsibilities do you have that may make it more difficult for you to complete your education? What resources, support, and encouragement do your spouse, family, and friends offer to you? Will you need to attend seminary close to where you currently live, or will you be able to relocate to attend a seminary that may not be close to where you are? Are there possibilities for online education that you can consider as one way to augment your education?

What are the advantages and disadvantages to you if you take the seminary route for ordination (¶324.4, a-c *Discipline,*), the optional route for deacon in full connection (¶324.5), or the Course of Study route for licensing (¶¶315.2, 318.1,2), or ordination (¶324.6)? Be sure that you understand the requirements of the *Discipline* and your annual conference for each of these.

Gender-related Issues for Reflection

Ideally, whether an individual is male or female should make no difference in career choices and effectiveness as a licensed or ordained minister. It is clear that it makes no difference in God's relation to individuals (see Galatians 3:28).

In reality, however, we are an imperfect church progressing toward this ideal. The traditional bias has been that licensed or ordained ministers are men. This is changing; and both men and women considering licensed or ordained ministry today have the opportunity to help shape these changes in constructive ways.

Some doors have opened, yet further growth will be needed in order to give fully equal opportunities to both women and men in licensed or ordained ministry.

Reflect how you think that being a man in ministry will affect your opportunities? Your ministry style? Your work with those you serve in congregations or other settings?

Reflect how you think that being a woman in ministry will affect your opportunities? Your ministry style? Your work with those you serve in congregations or other settings?

As a woman, how do you feel about possible gender biases that you may encounter as a licensed or ordained minister? Give an example of how you respond to these situations and how your response might help positively influence such biases.

How would it feel for you as a man or a woman to serve under the authority of an ordained woman as your senior pastor, district superintendent, or bishop?

Discuss with your mentor how you, as a man or a woman in ordained or licensed ministry, can contribute constructively to diminish stereotypes and to help the church move toward the goal of fully equal opportunities for women and men in ministry.

Have you observed differences in the reactions and responses of clergy and lay in your annual conference to the leadership between male and female district superintendents and bishops? How?

Discuss with your mentor how you will work to show equal respect, without deference to one sex or the other; and to avoid or discourage sexually compromising remarks or actions? What experiences have you had that would support your answer?

Your candidacy mentor may ask for additional information pertaining to one or more of the issues in these studies. This may involve additional educational evaluations, observations from others with whom you have worked, interviews with clergy members, additional interviews with you and your spouse or family, and other sources of information that may help you and the church to arrive at the best possible decisions concerning your candidacy.

It is more effective to deal adequately with these issues in this exploring stage of candidacy rather than delay until you meet with the district or board committee, or until later in your licensed or ordained ministry.

Gifts you Bring Through Vocational Change and Bi-Vocational Ministry

Several career transition situations are presented below with relevant information and questions. Select the ones that pertain to your circumstance to discuss with your candidacy mentor.

Making a Change from a Previous Career

In a sense, all of the apostles Jesus called made career changes (See Matthew 4:18-22). Perhaps the most dramatic career change was in Paul's conversion experience (Acts 9:1-31).

As you read these accounts afresh, consider the gifts that you bring to licensed or ordained ministry from your own previous career experiences and evaluate how your previous work experiences will influence your ministry.

What work skills, patterns, factors, or experiences from your former career will enhance or improve your decision about licensed or ordained ministry?

What work skills, patterns, factors, or experiences may detract from or diminish your ministry?

What experiences suggest to you that you will be more satisfied with a vocation in licensed or ordained ministry?

Choose to explore the situations and issues in this chapter that fit your circumstance, or adapt the questions to fit your circumstance.

The candidacy mentor is encouraged to be flexible and adjust the procedures and conversations to enable you to obtain maximum benefit.

Has it been necessary for you to conform to undesirable expectations of work conditions, fellow employees, or your managers or other work superiors? If so, how do you perceive these aspects will be different for you if you enter licensed or ordained ministry?

Usually a licensed or ordained minister must work comfortably and cooperatively in a variety of work settings with different management styles and with various persons in authority, such as bishop, district superintendent, members of the local church P/SPRC, administrative or other boards of directors, ministry supervisors, and others. In what ways are these relationships similar or different from your current work relationships?

If you were judged ineffective in your current or former employment/career and if your ineffectiveness is/was partly a result of your own behavior or work performance, to what extent are you able and willing to change your behavior to become more effective in areas that will also impact your effectiveness in ministry? What constructive changes have you already made?

Were there factors contributing to your ineffectiveness, such as health, family conflict, job conditions? How have you dealt these?

Regardless of your age, a second-career person entering licensed or ordained ministry may begin at an entry-level appointment. To some extent your maturity and experience as a second-career person will offset the tendency for others to treat you as a beginner or rookie in a new career.

There may be times when you will need additional patience and understanding as you deal with others whom you will meet in the Church structure of relationships. If you have not already done so, talk with a deacon, elder, or local pastor in an entry-level appointment and record any concerns you may discover.

If you have held positions that provide some measure of authority over others along with support services, ready access to equipment and resources, or influence in policy decisions, how important are these and other evidences of your former status to you now?

Early Retirement and Entry into a New Career

Some people discern a call to ministry or take the opportunity to answer a call to ministry after taking early retirement from a former career path. Many of the questions in the section above may also apply to you in this situation.

Some with other income are willing to serve appointments that do not pay as much. In other cases, however, a person may equate salary with success in the new career, so income may become one way to measure acceptance and success.

Conversely, churches may sometimes unfairly expect a second-career person with non-parish sources of income to serve at a lower salary. You may need to consider in depth the more subtle meanings of money and salary for you, your family, and for the ministry setting and annual conference in which you may serve.

If you have income from retirement or other benefits, to what extent will this be important to you in determining your appointment and income as a licensed or ordained minister?

List other issues you want to reflect with your candidacy mentor as you retire from one career and prepare to enter a vocation in licensed or ordained ministry.

Ordained Ministry as a Concurrent Vocation

The term second career usually refers to entering into licensed or ordained ministry after having been in another profession or line of work for some years.

Concurrent vocation or career refers to working in another occupation at the same time one is doing paid work in ordained ministry. In some settings it may be possible to serve in ministry and to also work part-time in other employment.

In what ways does your paid work experience affect your identity and your discernment of God's calling now? Many who are concerned about the future of churches with small membership and churches in rural, inner-city, and other communities suggest that the bi-vocational (part-time) elder is a primary method for providing ordained ministers to these parishes. Part-time ordained clergy may also provide much needed and effective ministries to other specialized ministries.

If you want to explore some type of concurrent career arrangement as a possibility in your annual conference, discuss this with your candidacy mentor and with others who can assist you in obtaining further information about how this can be done.

From Homemaker to a Vocation in Licensed or Ordained Ministry

If you have never worked outside your home, your family may have some difficulty in coping with your new commitment and revised priorities for your time and energy. Depending upon your family customs and habits, they may miss some of the many things that homemakers typically do for their families. On the other hand, some spouses and children may be even more pleased with a parent who is now a student and future licensed or ordained minister, and they may make a special effort to support her or him in this new vocational venture.

What are your feelings about changing to paid work outside the home? Do you have a sense that "Since you volunteer so much time already, you might as well be paid for it"?

What are the reactions of your own family members as you consider licensed or ordained ministry as a vocation?

What characteristics or skills have you developed out of your experiences in unpaid volunteer work? How have your volunteer experiences prepared you for further service in the world?

How will your future work as a licensed or ordained minister be similar or different from your volunteer work in the church and community?

How you interpret your life experiences and turn them and turn them into expectations for the future is a major key to your possible career change. You can bring many skills and insights from your successful experiences as a layperson to your future work as a licensed or ordained minister.

As you identify your strengths, limitations, and growth potentials in your previous career, discuss with your candidacy mentor how these may affect your work in licensed or ordained ministry. List the issues that are of greatest concern to you as you think about your career change. Discuss them with your candidacy mentor.

Diversity—A Gift to the Church

As a diverse people of God who bring special gifts and evidences of God's grace to the unity of the Church and to society, we are called to be faithful to the example of Jesus' ministry to all persons. Inclusiveness means openness, acceptance, and support that enable all persons to participate in the life of the Church, the community, and the world. (¶139, Discipline*)*

The United Methodist Church is committed to being an inclusive church. Your race, ethnicity, socioeconomic, language, and cultural background, greatly influence how you will minister to others.

Race and ethnicity

For the church's statement on the rights of racial and ethnic persons, read the Social Principles. (¶162 (A), *Discipline*)

Give illustrations of how your cultural heritage has given you insights and gifts that may be distinctly useful to your ordained or licensed ministry?

How does your racial or ethnic background influence your spiritual formation and identity? Do you believe you will be supported or find resources to continue your growth in spiritual formation in The United Methodist Church?

Describe a few experiences you have had with persons from a racial or ethnic group that is different from your own. Describe how they were positive or negative. How might these experiences influence your attitude or your effectiveness in licensed or ordained ministry?

How do you feel about serving persons whose racial and ethnic characteristics are different from your own?

How would you personally feel about serving in a cross-racial appointment where you are in the minority?

As a United Methodist licensed or ordained clergy person, you may have special opportunities to lead the Church toward its ideal for racial and ethnic inclusiveness. For example, you may be especially led to provide better models for racial and ethnic ministries. Your call and ability may allow you to challenge the dominant ethnic group to live more constructively as a truly inclusive church. You also may be called to develop some new models of multicultural ministry from your unique point of view. You can help all United Methodists and other Christians do ministry better in a world which is increasingly multiracial and multiethnic. Listen carefully to how God calls you to define your mission in the church?

Discuss with your mentor and note here any clues or direction about this that you have at this time in your discernment.

Socioeconomic and cultural background

Your socioeconomic and cultural background are related and include your place of residence, income level, type of occupation, family and community collective values, and other indicators.

Specific attitudes and values are not automatically associated with a certain socioeconomic status, although your specific type of background provides the context in which you formulate your attitudes, values, and life orientations. These in turn influence the ways that you carry out your ministry with persons from various socioeconomic and cultural backgrounds.

Socioeconomic Factors:

How does your socioeconomic background influence your spiritual formation and identity?

How might this be distinctly helpful to you in your licensed or ordained ministry setting? How might it hinder?

How might this influence your attitude or effectiveness in ministry in The United Methodist Church?

If you are from a family background in which you had modest or near-poverty level income, is the licensed or ordained ministry a way to secure a better income for yourself and your family?

If you are from a family background in which you had affluent or above-average income, will it be difficult for you to live on the salary that a typical licensed or ordained minister receives in The United Methodist Church?

Cultural Background:

In what kind of cultural background (rural, urban, suburban, international, etc.) was your spiritual identity formed?

What values have you discovered from your cultural background that you believe will positively impact your work as a licensed or ordained minister?

How would you personally feel about serving in a cross-cultural appointment whose cultural are distinctly different from your own?

As you consider your own racial or ethnic, socioeconomic, and cultural background (and, if you are married, the background of your spouse), reflect with your candidacy mentor on how you feel about serving various types of churches that are likely to be available to you in your annual conference (small rural church with less than 200 members, a county seat church with high community visibility, in-town neighborhood church, large suburban church, etc.)?

Language

Language-related issues appear in several ways in licensed or ordained ministry. In the United States, English is the primary language for conducting most annual conference and district meetings.

Whether formal English is your first language or not, it is important that you have good grammar, adequate vocabulary, and other language characteristics that make your ministry effective.

Are you willing to master a new language in order to minister to others, including new words, phrases, and slang terms in order to be more effective with children, youth, younger adults, or older adults?

If you are fluent in a non-English language, what is the positive way this can affect your ministry? Does it create limitations?

If you are not fluent in English, reflect how this will impact your ministry.

Your candidacy mentor may ask you to obtain additional information pertaining to one or more of these issues. This may involve additional educational evaluation, interviews with clergy from specific racial, ethnic, cultural or language groups, additional interviews with you and your spouse or family, and other sources of information that may help you and the church arrive at the best possible decisions concerning your candidacy.

Now is the time to deal with these issues rather than delay until you meet with the dCOM, or until later in your ministry.

Reflect on your insights from this study with your candidacy mentor. Close by giving thanks for your cultural inheritance and the way it contributes to your gifts for ministry.

From Gifts to Fruit: A Transition

Fruit is the result of God's grace made evident through our gifts. John Wesley's third set of questions to examiners (¶310, *Discipline*) asks: "Have they fruit? Have any been truly convinced of sin and converted to God, and are believers edified by their service?"

Review the passage in Galatians 5:22-23a that identifies the fruits of the Spirit as love, joy, peace, patience, kindness, generosity, faithfulness, gentleness, self-control. Consider also Jesus' emphasis on fruit and its sources (for example, Matthew 7:17-19, 12:33, and parallels) and Paul's emphasis on lifestyle and faith (for example, Romans 12, 1 Corinthians 13). Note in the margin fruits of the Spirit from your review of the scripture.

The "fruit of the Spirit" is the evidence of the Holy Spirit at work in your life. John Wesley believed the evidence in Christian living is to be found in changes in both faith and behavior, demonstrated through a person's love of God and love of neighbor and through service to the community.

With your candidacy mentor, consider evidences of God's Spirit at work in your life now and seek to identify the links of fruit with grace and gifts.

Recognizing Your Fruits Through Service

In your journey as a Christian, you have probably been involved in many projects and activities that reach out in ministry to other persons or groups within the church and outside the church.

Active service to others unites gifts and fruit. John Wesley and his early followers in the Oxford Club met regularly for prayer and study in the mornings and in the afternoon visited those who were sick, in prison, and in other conditions needing their ministries.

Biblical Views of Spiritual Formation and Service

In the Bible and throughout the history of the church one's Christian personhood and formation has usually been seen in the tension and balance between faith and works. Active service for Christ is an expression of inner spiritual qualities and at the same time reaches out to serve and to witness the Christ to others in the name of the church. Select a service ministry in which you are currently involved and reflect on how it is forming you spiritually.

How is it an expression of your God-given gifts?

Read and discuss one of these biblical views of service and spirituality with your candidacy mentor.
- Luke 10:29-37; Luke 15:3-32. In these parables, Jesus urges us to take action on the basis of our commitment.
- Hebrews 11; James 1-3. The point and counterpoint between faith and action is emphasized repeatedly in these passages.
- 1 Timothy 1-5. Paul's instructions to Timothy as a minister of Jesus Christ are still appropriate for us today.

In these and other biblical passages, we are reminded to act for Christ, reflect on that action, and evaluate its effectiveness according to Christ's standards of love, so that we can return to action. The scriptures see the formation of our spirits as intimately related to active service to others in the name of Christ. Actions emerge from the way a person's spirit has been formed, and spiritual formation results from action.

Session 7 in *Understanding God's Call: A Ministry Inquiry Process* on the United Methodist Heritage of uniting faith and good works might be helpful as you reflect on the fruits of the spirit.

Discerning Your Fruit Through Successes and Failures

Since this chapter invites you to identify some successes and some failures you have experienced, begin by clarifying what makes a project, event, or relationship a success or failure to you.

The judgment of success or failure involves some type of standard or criteria against which you measure a specific project or service. It also involves viewpoints of yourself, others involved, observers, and those whose views you respect or whose approval you desire.

As you discuss the following issues with your candidacy mentor, consider what you have learned about your own journey, character, gifts, and fruits.

Successes in Ministry

Success may be reaching a certain number or type of persons, receiving favorable comments, seeing individuals change, increasing involvement of others, or signs of nurture and growth in other persons.

Successes in Ministry and Their Impact on you

Describe a situation in which your witness for Christ had a significant effect on another person.

How do you define success in licensed or ordained ministry?

How do you measure success in ways that others can also observe?

What is the role of the Christian community (local church, supervisors, colleagues, and constituents) in identifying and celebrating successful ministries?

Describe one or two successful projects in which you were involved as a leader, including initial planning and preparation, the event itself, and post-event follow-up.

Describe the project and define what you mean by successful in this project.

What was your role in the project? What plans did you make? In what ways did you enable others to become involved in the project?

How did you cope with disagreements, disappointments, or surprises?

How have these outcomes influenced your spiritual growth and understanding of your gifts, talents, and promise as a licensed or ordained minister?

What does this experience tell you about the fruits of your faith and does it validate your awareness of God's calling to you?

Failures in Ministry

Failure may be a matter of not reaching a desired goal, being embarrassed, causing conflict, or lack of participation in some way. Failure may be in your own judgment or in the evaluation of others.

Failures in Ministry and Their Impact on you

Describe a situation in which you feel that your witness for Christ did not have any effect on another person.

How do you define failure in licensed or ordained ministry?

How do you measure failure in ways that others can also observe?

What is the role of the Christian community (local church, supervisors, colleagues, and constituents) in evaluating failed or inefficient attempts at ministry?

Describe one or two unsuccessful projects in which you were involved as a leader, including initial planning and preparation, the event itself, and post-event follow-up.

Describe the project and what you mean by failure in relation to it.

How do you react to being unable to accomplish a worthy goal?

What would you do differently if you were to do a similar project again?

How has this experience shaped your own spirit or helped you grow?

What does this experience tell you about the fruits of your faith?

Feedback from Others who Know you Well

Interview two or three people who know you well. Ask them for sincere and honest feedback about what gifts they think you have or may develop for licensed or ordained ministry. How have they seen those gifts bearing fruit by touching the lives of others? Record insights, surprises, and appreciations from these interviews.

From Exploring to Declared Candidate: A Transition

During this period of exploration and discernment about your call to licensed or ordained ministry, you have considered your grace, gifts, and fruit for ministry. Talk with your candidacy mentor about how you would now answer John Wesley's questions for examiners (¶310, *Discipline*) as a way to bring closure to this phase of your candidacy studies.

Grace: Do they know God as a pardoning God? Have they the love of God abiding in them? Do they desire nothing but God? Are they holy in all manner of conversation?

Gifts: Have they gifts, as well as evidence of God's grace, for the work? Have they a clear, sound understanding; a right judgment in the things of God; a just conception of salvation by faith? Do they speak justly, readily, clearly?

Fruit: Have they fruit? Have any been truly convinced of sin and converted to God, and are believers edified by their service?

Wesley concludes, "As long as these marks occur in them, we believe they are called of God to serve. These we receive as sufficient proof that they are moved by the Holy Spirit."

Making Decisions–
Reviewing Ministry Options

The purpose of this chapter is to give you the opportunity to clarify any remaining questions about the nature and requirements of license and ordained ministry in The United Methodist Church as you prepare to publicly declare your call to licensed or ordained ministry.

See Appendix E (pg. 227) *Understanding God's Call: A Ministry Inquiry Process* for a more thorough discussion about ministry options.

Begin this time of discernment with this prayer or one of your own choosing.

> *O God, we realize that you do not call us to be successful in the marketplace; you call us to be faithful as disciples of Jesus. You do not call us to achievement in work, but to responsible living. You do not call us to make a great fortune, but to labor for your reign. Guide us into greater understanding of your priorities. Amen.*

From *The United Methodist Book of Worship*, No. 539. Reprinted with the permission of The Pilgrim Press.

Reviewing Ministry Options

The Meaning of Ordination

If you have not done so, you are encouraged to read Section I in "The Ministry of the Ordained" (¶¶301-305 and ¶138, *Discipline*).

With your mentor discuss the meaning of ordination, clergy orders, and conference membership in The United Methodist Church.

What is your understanding of ordination? How would you tell someone what it means?

Draw on your own experience to describe your understanding of the ministries of ordained elder, ordained deacon, and local pastor.

History of Ministry Orders

The history of the deacon and the history of the elder are found in Appendix B at the back of this book. You may record questions about the history of the orders of ordained ministry here for discussion with your candidacy mentor.

The Ministry of Elder

If you have not done so, you are encouraged to read ¶¶332-334 in the *Discipline* about the church's understanding of "The Ministry of an Elder."

Talk with your mentor about the understanding of the ministry of an elder in these paragraphs.

You are encouraged to interview an elder about her or his understanding of ministry. Ask questions such as: Why do you believe the ministry of an elder is your most faithful response to God's call? What kind of ministry do you have? What are the benefits of the ministry of an elder? What are the challenges? What special qualities or skills are needed for this kind of ministry?

If you were to enter the ministry of an elder in response to God's call, how would your ministry be expressed through your vocation?

Surviving and Thriving in the Itinerant System

With your candidacy mentor, review the procedure and assumptions involved in the United Methodist itinerant system for elders. (¶¶337-338, and 343-344, *Discipline*).

Discuss the ways that the procedure and assumptions are typically expressed in your annual conference and your response to that.

Discuss what reactions your family has to these procedures, especially if they are considerably different from the current ways that you determine your work setting and housing?

How comfortable are you with having some other authority, even if in consultation with you, determine whether you will remain or move from a community and church that you enjoy?

How has the United Methodist itinerant system influenced your decision regarding licensed or ordained ministry?

The Ministry of a Deacon in Full Connection

If you have not done so, you are encouraged to read ¶¶328-329, and 331 in the *Discipline* about the church's understanding of "The Ministry of a Deacon."

Talk with your mentor about the understanding of the ministry of a deacon in these paragraphs.

You are encouraged to interview a deacon in full connection about his or her understanding of ministry. Ask questions such as: Why do you believe the ministry of a deacon in full connection is a faithful response to God's call? What kind of ministry do you have? What are the benefits of this ministry? What are the challenges? What special qualities or skills are needed for this kind of ministry?

If you were to enter the ministry of a deacon in response to God's call, how would your ministry be expressed through your vocation?

Understanding the Appointment System for Deacons

With your candidacy mentor, review the procedure and assumptions involved in the United Methodist appointment system for deacons. (¶331, *Discipline*)

Discuss the understanding you have about the categories of deacon appointments and how deacons receive their appointments.

Discuss your understanding about primary and secondary appointments for deacons. What does each mean?

If you become an ordained deacon are you comfortable with the understanding that deacons are not part of the itinerant system and the bishop is not obligated to continue you under an annual appointment in the same way as an elder?

The Ministry of a Licensed Local Pastor

If you have not done so, you are encouraged to read ¶¶315-316 in the *Discipline* about the church's understanding of "License for Pastoral Ministry."

Talk with your mentor about the understanding of the ministry of a licensed local pastor in these paragraphs.

Discuss the distinction between a licensed local pastor and an ordained elder even though both serve to pastor local churches.

If you were to enter the ministry of licensed local pastor in response to God's call, how would your ministry be expressed through your vocation?

Making Decisions - Next Steps

Call to Licensed or Ordained Ministry

Compare your sense of call from when you began formally exploring a call to ministry to now. How has your understanding of the call to licensed or ordained ministry changed?

Your Decision

Although your decision concerning some form of licensed or ordained ministry is eventually yes or no, many factors help to shape it. You may benefit from listing the factors that favor a decision to enter licensed or ordained ministry and the issues or concerns that do not favor such a decision.

Favor	Do Not Favor

On the basis of the factors you have reviewed, you have three possibilities: yes, maybe, and no. As you look at these possibilities, it is vitally important that you make a decision that is right for you as you understand yourself in relation to God's grace and call to you.

As you grow in your understanding with others and with God, you may decide to change your current decision. Decisions are subject to revision because decisions lead to more decisions. Thus you may decide no now, but later change to a yes. You may decide yes now, but later change to a maybe or no. After you have made this decision, you may want to offer it to God, "God, is this what you want?"

"No" as an Option

If the answer is no, what kind of thoughts and feelings does this raise?

Now that you have explored licensed or ordained ministry in depth as a possible vocation, you may decide that your Christian work is in the ministry of the laity. If no is your decision regarding licensed or ordained ministry, your candidacy mentor and church will support you fully in your decision.

You can apply the process of self-discovery that you have learned in this candidacy process to investigate other possible careers as your response to God's grace and love as a layperson in ministry in the church.

If you answer no at this step in the candidacy process, you can always return at a later time if you desire to explore again the licensed or ordained ministry as your Christian vocation. You may also want to discuss other career issues with your candidacy mentor, and later let your candidacy mentor know of your subsequent plans and decisions.

Create a way for remembering the journey you have traveled together with your candidacy mentor and pray together for the journey ahead as you move into new relationships and new ventures in ministry.

"Maybe" as an Option

If the answer is maybe, what kind of thoughts and feelings does this raise?

After several interviews and exploration, you may still be undecided about whether to become a declared candidate for ordained ministry. If you are still in high school or in the early part of college study, you may want to obtain additional life experiences before you decide definitely. Some persons may have completed college and still be uncertain about commitment to a career in licensed or ordained ministry.

In any career decision, there is often some element of uncertainty or reluctance. You may ask others if they have experienced this in their vocational decisions. This uncertainty is part of life and due to the fact that we cannot precisely predict the future. As Christians, however, we can be confident that God holds the future and will be with us as we continue living toward it.

In this exploratory vocational process, you may have found a lot of uncertainty in your life. Discuss where you are now in your decision with your candidacy mentor and whether your maybe is an appropriate decision for you at this time in your life.

You may want to arrange for further discussions with your candidacy mentor or with other persons as you continue to clarify your vocational plans. Explore ways in which the candidacy mentor can be of further assistance in guiding you to the decision point.

"Yes" as an Option

If the answer is yes, what kind of thoughts and feelings does this raise?

If you have come to a yes decision about declaring your candidacy in the local church and requesting the support of your charge conference, you may wish to discuss the role of the Pastor/Staff Parish Relations Committee (P/SPRC), the charge conference, and the dCOM in the decision-making process with your candidacy mentor. The next section of this book will guide you more specifically through that process.

Your request to the local church and the dCOM does not guarantee that you will be confirmed as a candidate for licensed or ordained ministry. You are offering yourself to the church for its consideration.

Your decision to seek certification as a candidate is one of two basic decisions involved. The other decision is on behalf of the church by its local church and district representatives as they decide, by your grace, gifts, and fruit, whether the church can be served well by inviting you into its licensed or ordained ministry.

Share with your candidacy mentor your decision about seeking certification as a candidate for ordained ministry and the discernment process that led you to that decision.

Following this decision, it is appropriate to celebrate with your mentor, observing and honoring what you have discovered and asking for God's direction as you continue the journey of the candidacy process to licensed or ordained ministry.

Section 3:
Declaring Candidacy

Declaring your Call to Licensed or Ordained Ministry

Declaring your candidacy involves consultation with your local church pastor and pastor/staff parish relations committee (P/SPRC) or other recognized United Methodist ministry setting about a recommendation from your charge conference or other body specified by the district committee to the dCOM.

To guide your reflection about your grace, gifts, and fruit as you prepare to declare your candidacy, begin your time together with this prayer or another of your choosing:

> *We heed, O Lord, your summons,*
> *And answer: Here are we!*
> *Send us upon your errand,*
> *Let us your servants be.*
> *Our strength is dust and ashes,*
> *Our years a passing hour;*
> *But you can use our weakness*
> *To magnify your power.*
> *Help us God to hear you;*
> *And give us the courage to follow you.*
> *Amen*

The words above, except the last two lines, are from the hymn, *The Voice of God is Calling*, verse 3. *The United Methodist Hymnal*, No. 436. Used by permission.

Recommendation by Local Ministry Setting

In this stage of the candidacy process, it is assumed that:

1. You have made a decision to pursue ordination as a deacon or as an elder, or license as a local pastor, and

2. You are ready to make this decision public to your local setting in ministry and the dCOM.

Your role at this stage of the process is to share what you have learned about God's grace, gifts, and your fruit with your pastor and P/SPRC or equivalent in ministry setting and ask for their recommendation to the charge conference or equivalent as specified by the dCOM. Your candidacy mentor will guide you in this process as defined in the *Book of Discipline* of The United Methodist Church:

> *Those beginning candidacy for licensed or ordained ministry following their one-year membership; their enrollment in online candidacy; and assignment of a candidacy mentor: (¶311.1d, e)*
>
> - *shall write their statement of call and responses to Wesley's historic questions in ¶310. The candidate will consult with the pastor or equivalent in their ministry setting to request a meeting of the pastor parish relations committee or equivalent to consider the statement of call and Wesley's historic questions;*
>
> - *After approval of the candidate by pastor parish relations committee or equivalent, shall meet with a charge conference or body specified by the district committee on ordained ministry called to recommend the candidate to the district committee on ordained ministry. Approval of the candidate must be by two-thirds written ballot.*

Reflection with Candidacy Mentor

1. Discuss with your candidacy mentor how best to express your relationship to God and your discernment of God's call to the committee in your local ministry setting. Note ideas here:

2. Write a draft of a letter to your pastor and local committee asking to be recommended for candidacy for licensed or ordained ministry. Include your statement of call in your letter. Discuss the letter with your candidacy mentor and make any needed changes before writing a final draft. **Keep a copy of all documents for your own records.**

3. Write out answers to Wesley's historic questions (¶310, *Discipline*) that reflect your relationship to God and your call to licensed or ordained ministry and discuss them with your candidacy mentor. It may take several drafts to state your beliefs clearly.

Meeting with Your Pastor

You probably have already talked with your pastor or campus minister about your progress in the candidacy studies. If you have not this meeting will also include some opportunity to describe your experiences and perhaps give some reasons for the sequence of steps you have chosen thus far.

Once you have sent a letter asking for a recommendation, arrange with your pastor details of the meetings with the local committees.

Your pastor or campus minister is a key person. She or he can provide important information about the structure of the local church, district, and annual conference that can assist you in your progress toward licensed or ordained ministry as your Christian vocation.

Reflection with Candidacy Mentor

1. Rehearse with your candidacy mentor what you need to discuss with your pastor in your meeting. Make a list of questions you need to ask.

In preparation for this meeting, write a draft or revise a previous statement of call making sure it reflects grace, gifts, and fruits as you have discerned them in your candidacy studies.

2. Make a list of any proposals you would like to make as you meet with the local committee, such as a request to meet with the chairperson of the P/SPRC or local committee to clarify the purpose of the meeting and the expectations of the committee; your desire to make a brief beginning statement to the committee; or that you will provide copies of the documents for each member of the committee in advance. There is no prescribed format for this meeting other than they are asked to discuss Wesley's historic questions about grace, gifts, and fruit with you. (¶310, *Discipline*)

Meeting with the P/SPRC or Local Committee

The members of the committee may have had experience in matters directly relating to licensed or ordained ministry as they have worked with the pastor and other staff (if any) and they have also had contacts with the district superintendent. They can bring this knowledge to assist you as they consider whether or not to recommend you for licensed or ordained ministry.

As outlined in *The Christian as Minister*, the P/SPRC or local committee is charged with the responsibility of deciding on behalf of the local church and The United Methodist Church whether to recommend you as a declared candidate. Every licensed or ordained minister in the church has received this recommendation at the beginning of her or his work toward ordination or licensing.

The P/SPRC or local committee must decide whether you have the initial grace, gifts, fruit, and promise for effectiveness in licensed or ordained ministry. One way of testing this is to consider whether they would like to have you as their pastor, assuming that you had the training and experience needed.

The committee is encouraged not to give a yes vote lightly. If your calling and decision are valid, both can stand the test of careful inquiry and examination. Indeed, this can be a welcome strengthening of your own insights, as well as an expression of the committee's pastoral care and concern for you.

Reflection with Candidacy Mentor

1. Rehearse with your candidacy mentor what you most want to communicate in your meeting with the P/SPRC or local committee.

2. If you make an opening statement, keep it brief. Write here what you would want to say.

3. Review questions for the committee suggested in *The Christian as Minister* with your candidacy mentor.

4. Think through strategies for moments when you might get stuck, e.g., your mind goes blank, you don't understand a question, or a member of the committee is challenging you theologically. What will you do if committee members seem to run out of questions? Try to imagine some possibilities so you can handle yourself with confidence and grace.

Meeting with your Charge Conference (or the body specified by the dCOM)

Several suggestions are offered in *The Christian as Minister* concerning your meeting with your charge conference and its potential recommendation of you as a declared candidate. You will want to read Chapter 3: "Steps Into Servant Leadership" and Chapter 5: "Guidelines for the Pastor/Staff Parish Relations Committee" as a way of preparing for your appearance before the charge conference.

The Procedure

1. With your pastor, clarify the procedure at the charge conference. What is expected of you? Are you to speak, and if so when, and about what? This may be a review of the proposals that you made at the meeting with your pastor.

2. With your candidacy mentor, rehearse what you will say and do at the charge conference.

3. Take with you a copy of your "Declaration of Candidacy for Ordained Ministry" (see the following page in this guidebook.) Sign Part I of the declaration yourself and have the district superintendent sign Part II once you have received the support and recommendation of the charge conference.

THE UNITED METHODIST CHURCH
DECLARATION OF CANDIDACY FOR ORDAINED MINISTRY
RECOMMENDATION OF CHARGE CONFERENCE or EQIVALENT DETERMINED BY dCOM

I hereby declare my candidacy for ordained ministry in The United Methodist Church and request the support and recommendation of the Charge Conference or equivalent for certification as a candidate for:

Order of Deacons _____ Order of Elders _____ License as Local Pastor _____

Signed _____ Date _____
        Signature of the Declared Candidate

II. RECOMMENDATION OF CHARGE CONFERENCE OR EQUIVALENT

Let those who consider recommending persons for candidacy as ordained ministers in The United Methodist Church ask themselves the following questions which were first asked by John Wesley at the third conference of Methodist preachers in 1746.

1. Do they know God as a pardoning God? Have they the love of God abiding in them? Do they desire nothing but God? Are they holy in all manner of conversation?

2. Have they gifts, as well as grace, for the work? Have they a clear, sound understanding; a right judgment in the things of God; a just conception of salvation by faith? Do they speak justly, readily, clearly?

3. Have they fruit? (To Elder and Local Pastor) Have any been truly convinced of sin and converted to God, and are believers edified by their preaching? (To Deacon) Are others edified by their service?

Believing that _____ is called of God and is a suitable candidate for ordained ministry in The United Methodist Church, the Charge Conference or equivalent of _____ recommends him/her for certification as a candidate by the district Committee on Ordained Ministry. In making this recommendation, we attest to the fact that the declared candidate has been a member or affiliate member of the charge for at least one year, has graduated from an accredited high school or received a certificate of equivalency, and has received by written ballot a two-thirds vote of the charge conference.

Signed _____ Date _____
        Signature of authorized elder, district superintendent, or bishop

Conference _____ District _____

(Further instructions on reverse side of page.)   **Form 104/2008**

This Declaration of Candidacy for Ordained Ministry should be sent to the district Committee on Ordained Ministry along with:

1. A written response to the following by the candidate:
   a. the most formative experience of your Christian life;
   b. God's call to ordained ministry and the role of the church in your call;
   c. your personal beliefs as a Christian;
   d. your gifts for ministry;
   e. your present understanding of call to ministry as elder, deacon, or licensed ministry; and
   d. your support system.
2. Provide other information as may be required for determining gifts, evidence of God's grace, fruit, and demonstration of the call for the ministry of deacon or elder; and
3. Agree for the sake of the mission of Jesus Christ in the world and the most effective witness of the gospel, and in consideration of their influence as ministers, to make a complete dedication of themselves to the highest ideals of the Christian life as set forth in ¶¶102-104, ¶¶160-166. To this end agree to exercise responsible self-control by personal habits conducive to bodily health, mental and emotional maturity, fidelity in marriage and celibacy in singleness, social responsibility, and growth in grace and the knowledge and love of God.
4. Complete and release required psychological reports, criminal background, and credit checks.

This form can be found at www.gbhem.org/candidacy/forms

The District Committee Process

Consult with your candidacy mentor about other specific requirements in your annual conference that are beyond these required by the *Book of Discipline*.

Now that you have declared your candidacy for licensed or ordained ministry, your candidacy mentor will help you prepare for meeting with the dCOM in a process to become a certified candidate for licensed or ordained ministry.

Requirements for certified candidacy

As you collect and write these documents, draw on the expertise of your candidacy mentor and pastor, particularly in the content and format of the written documents.

According to ¶311.2, *Discipline*:

> *Candidates approved by the charge conference and seeking to become certified for licensed or ordained ministry shall:*
> *1) Request to meet with the dCOM. In preparation for meeting with the district committee, provide the following written information, in addition to the responses previously written to Wesley's historic questions on grace, gifts, and fruit.*
>> *a) What is the most formative experience of your Christian life?*
>> *b) Describe God's call to licensed or ordained ministry and the role of the church in your call.*
>> *c) Write about your beliefs as a Christian.*
>> *d) Describe your gifts for ministry.*
>> *e) Describe your present understanding of your call to ministry as elder, deacon, or licensed ministry.*
>> *f) Describe your support system.*
>
> *2) Complete and release required psychological reports, criminal background and credit checks. Submit, on a form provided by the conference board of ordained ministry:*
>> *a) a notarized statement detailing any convictions for felony or misdemeanor or written accusations of sexual misconduct or child abuse; or*
>> *b) a notarized statement certifying that you have neither been accused in writing nor convicted of a felony, misdemeanor, any incident of sexual misconduct, or child abuse.*
>
> *3) Provide other information as the district committee may require for determining gifts, evidence of God's grace, fruit, and demonstration of the call to licensed or ordained ministry.*

4) Agree for the sake of the mission of Jesus Christ in the world and the most effective witness of the gospel, and in consideration of your influence as clergy, to make a complete dedication to the highest ideals of the Christian life as set forth in ¶¶ 102-104; 160-166. To this end you will agree to exercise responsible self-control by personal habits conducive to bodily health, mental and emotional maturity, fidelity in marriage and celibacy in singleness, social responsibility, and growth in grace and the knowledge and love of God.

Preparing for Meeting with the District Committee on Ordained Ministry

The dCOM has responsibility for supervising "all matters dealing with candidacy for the ordained ministry and with the license for local pastor." (¶665.5, *Discipline*) The dCOM maintains continuing contact, records, and review of candidates until they become associate members or provisional members of the annual conference (¶665.7, *Discipline*).

Like your local committees, the dCOM must be concerned about the best interests of The United Methodist Church and its licensed or ordained ministry. Lay members of The United Methodist Church make judgments about persons in the candidacy process through the local committees. The dCOM, which is composed of both ordained ministers and laypersons, provides the judgment of ordained ministers about candidates for licensed or ordained ministry. Contributions from both lay and ordained persons are important in the decision to accept an individual as a candidate for licensed or ordained ministry.

Four Parties are Involved in Your Meeting with the dCOM

1. You–the person requesting certification.
2. The candidacy mentor.
3. The district superintendent.
4. The members of the dCOM.

Some suggestions to you in relation to each of these parties are provided here.

1. The person requesting certification

Now that you have been recommended by your local church or other local entity, you and your candidacy mentor will discuss the appropriate preparation that you need to make for your meeting with the dCOM.

Your conversations with the candidacy mentor and files are confidential. Any information from them is to be released only with your written permission. This is why the candidacy mentor's report is to be available to you early enough that any changes may be made prior to the dCOM meeting. The dCOM is not to request information from those interviews not contained in your candidacy mentor's report. However, you may voluntarily include any of this information yourself.

In addition to the documents you prepare, your candidacy mentor will prepare a report about your progress and experiences in the exploratory studies you have completed. Prior to the meeting with the dCOM, you will have opportunity to read your candidacy mentor's statements about you and to discuss any questions or modifications that may be appropriate. This report is your candidacy mentor's public statement to the committee on your behalf. It is important that you and your candidacy mentor reach a consensus in this report. Remember that any information in the mentor report is to be released only with your written permission.

In the meeting with the dCOM, you will have an opportunity to add any comments or clarifications that you consider necessary concerning this report. The committee may ask either you or your candidacy mentor for further clarifications.

If you have any questions or concerns about any detail of this process, be sure to discuss these with your candidacy mentor. Each district may have certain procedures that are not specified in these *Guidelines*, and your candidacy mentor can provide a written statement of these additional procedures.

Make notes here about questions you have about your preparation for this meeting:

Make notes here for your introductory statement to the dCOM:

2. The Candidacy Mentor

Your candidacy mentor will provide details for the procedure for working with the dCOM concerning your certification as a candidate. If you feel uncertain or overwhelmed by this meeting, talk about your feelings with your candidacy mentor.

The candidacy mentor's discernment report provides an introduction of you to the dCOM and is to be available to you prior to the meeting with the dCOM. This gives information both to the dCOM and to you concerning your progress in the exploratory studies.

The report of your candidacy mentor to the dCOM can include areas such as these:

- A brief description of your grace, gifts, fruit, and promise for effectiveness in licensed or ordained ministry as mutually agreed upon by you and the mentor.
- The ways you have obtained information about the ministry of the deacon, the ministry of the elder, and the ministry of the local pastor.
- Ways you have used information in developing your understanding of yourself and licensed or ordained ministry.
- Other insights or comments about you that may enable the dCOM to understand you better.

As introductory and informational, the report should be brief and useful, but it should not contain any confidential information without your permission. The report is signed by both you and the candidacy mentor and will be shared with the dCOM with respect for the confidential nature of the relationship.

The dCOM will use the report as one source of information and will obtain additional information through the process which has been established by the committee and the annual conference board.

Your candidacy mentor is encouraged to be present with you in the meeting with the dCOM to present the report and to observe the interaction between you and the committee. The candidacy mentor is expected to be only an observer (after the initial report) so that the members of the committee can talk directly with you and you with them.

Your candidacy mentor is not present to try to influence the vote of the committee about you. Your presentation of yourself and the documentation you submit are the primary criteria on which the dCOM will decide whether or not to certify you as a candidate for licensed or ordained ministry.

After the meeting with the committee, you and your candidacy mentor should meet to discuss the interview and your understanding of the committee's recommendations and comments. If the dCOM offers suggestions or sets conditions that you must complete, you can talk with your candidacy mentor and make necessary arrangements to fulfill these requirements. Your candidacy mentor should also attach a record of the vote and any comments or recommendations of the dCOM to the report that was prepared to introduce you.

Make notes here about any questions you want to ask your candidacy mentor about her or his role in this certification of candidacy process.

3. The district superintendent

You may have already met with your district superintendent when you requested to enroll in candidacy or at other times. If not, it is helpful to have some contact in person or by telephone with your district superintendent prior to meeting with the dCOM. While the candidacy mentor continues contact with candidates on behalf of the dCOM, you are welcome to see your district superintendent any time you need clarification or assistance in your candidacy process.

Some district superintendents arrange a public way to acknowledge the new status of certified candidates and present a certificate of candidacy. This service may be in the candidate's local setting or at a district meeting. You may consult with your district superintendent and others about whether this will be done in your case.

Make notes here about matters you want to discuss with your district superintendent:

4. The District Committee on Ordained Ministry

The dCOM must consider several criteria in the certification process, as set forth earlier in this chapter, page 128, and in the *Book of Discipline* (¶311.2). It is the dCOM that certifies you as a candidate for licensed or ordained ministry.

Expectations. The first priority of the dCOM is to find the best possible leadership for licensed or ordained ministry and the church. You may be asked to supply other information that relates to your grace, gifts, and fruit indicating your fitness for a vocation in the licensed or ordained ministry of The United Methodist Church.

Your dCOM may make such requests according to your needs and the committee's needs. Among these may be:

- an evaluation by a psychologist
- references from employers
- evidence of educational achievement
- interviews about you with other persons
- examples of your academic and church-related work
- observations of you in actual tasks that are related to the work of the church

In the meeting of the dCOM, it is intended that every person will be as open and candid about you and the candidacy process as possible, notwithstanding the confidential relationship between you and your candidacy mentor. With a flexible and positive attitude, you and the committee members can discuss any issues that are related to your request for certification. The members of the dCOM will want you to have time to express your understanding of yourself and of God's call and to describe your plans for continuing in the educational preparation for licensed or ordained ministry.

The discussion. During the meeting with the dCOM, you will find that the members are interested in you and your welfare, as well as being concerned to find the best licensed and ordained ministers possible. Although this will be an important meeting, the atmosphere should be informal, warm, and openly candid.

The discussions that committee members have with you may cover a variety of topics, most of which you have probably discussed earlier with your candidacy mentor. If questions or issues arise that are unfamiliar, you should give your best responses and feel comfortable in stating the limits or conditions of your answers. In these ways, the committee members can become better acquainted with you. If you are unclear about the purpose of any question, you should feel free to ask for clarification.

The deliberation. As a matter of annual conference policy, the dCOM will decide whether or not you are to be present during their deliberation.

The members of the dCOM will vote on your certification by written ballot, with a three-fourths majority being needed for approval (*Discipline*, ¶665.6). In addition, they will offer other suggestions or counsel, as well as give you a clear explanation of the reasons for their decision. The dCOM will give this information directly to you and your candidacy mentor.

The decision. The dCOM has three possible decisions it can make:

1) **Yes.** If the dCOM decides to certify you as a candidate for licensed or ordained ministry, the committee will inform you of the decision. It may offer you insights and suggestions based on the members' contacts with you. In addition, your candidacy mentor, district superintendent, pastor, and many others are available to you as consultants in your decisions about educational and continuing preparation for the licensed or ordained ministry.

2) **Deferred.** If the committee members have major uncertainties about you, it is important for them to delay a decision until any questions can be clarified. The committee may inform you that further information or other work will be necessary before a decision can be made. It is important to be clear and open with you and your candidacy mentor about the nature of the uncertainties and to offer appropriate counsel to you in the process.

3) **No.** If the dCOM decides not to certify you as a candidate, it should give reasons for this decision directly to you during or immediately following the committee meeting. The committee also can make suggestions to you about any subsequent options or decisions that you may have. Your candidacy mentor can also be available to help interpret opinions and alternatives for both you and the committee.

Reporting the decision. A form for reporting the decision of the dCOM about your candidacy is provided on page 136 in this guidebook (Form 113). The dCOM, in cooperation with the BOM, determines the details of the reporting procedure. In most instances, this completed form is the only report needed by the four involved persons listed.

Your candidacy mentor is asked to record the vote and recommendations of the dCOM at the appropriate site (www.canapply.gbhem.org) in the online enrollment procedure.

The mentor may also inform the following:

1) a copy for the annual conference registrar for candidacy
2) a copy for your records in the log of this guidebook, page 30
3) a copy for your candidacy mentor to keep

Reflection with your Candidacy Mentor

1. Reflect on your experience of declaring candidacy and applying for certification as a candidate with your candidacy mentor.

2. Where in this part of the process have you perceived God's presence?

District Committee on Ordained Ministry Approval Report
for Certified Candidate for Ordained Ministry

Name of Candidate _____

Address (School) _____
               Street   City   State   Zip

Address (Permanent) _____
               Street   City   State   Zip

E-mail: _____

Charge Conference _____

District _____

Annual Conference _____

Candidacy Mentor _____

Name of District Superintendent _____

Date received affirmative vote from Charge Conference _____

Date met the district Committee on Ordained Ministry _____

The candidate has completed *The Christian as Minister* and the first two chapters of the *Candidacy Guidebook* with a candidacy mentor.

Received Certification as a Candidate for:

☐ Order of Deacons   ☐ Order of Elders   ☐ License as Local Pastor   ☐ Chaplain
☐ Certification Delayed   ☐ Certification Denied

☐ During the candidacy studies the inquiring candidate decided not to continue a process toward ordained ministry as a vocation.

A certified candidate must complete a minimum of 1 year, maximum 12 years as certified candidate prior to probationary membership.

_____   _____
Signature of Candidacy Mentor   Date

Address (School) _____
               Street   City   State   Zip

This form is found and completed at the candidacy online enrollment Web site at www.gbhem.org/candidacy/forms.

Form 113/2008

From Declaring to Continuing Candidacy: A Transition

The next section of this Candidacy Guidebook is to be completed by candidates for ordained deacon or elder during your period of certified candidacy, which may last from "at least one (1) year and no more than twelve (12) years" (¶324.1, *Discipline*)

Discernment is not completed when you become a certified candidate. Every day is a process of discernment in terms of what God wants you to do with your life. The next section provides opportunities for discernment and evaluation during certified candidacy until you become licensed as a local pastor or commissioned as a provisional member.

Those persons who are approved as certified candidates and go on to complete licensing school, enroll in the prescribed Course of Study and are appointed as a licensed local pastor. They are clergy members of the annual conference (see ¶602.1) and are no longer certified candidates.

Licensed local pastors do not continue with candidacy mentors or with this guidebook. They will be assigned a clergy mentor by the district committee on ordained ministry in consultation with the district superintendent. (See ¶¶314 and 349.1b, *Discipline*) Resources for licensing school and Course of Study are found in the appendix.

Those persons who are approved as certified candidates, go on to complete licensing school, enroll in the prescribed Course of Study and are appointed as a licensed local pastor. They are clergy members of the annual conference (see ¶602.1) and are no longer certified candidates.

Licensed local pastors do not continue with candidacy mentors or with this guidebook. They will be assigned a clergy mentor by the district committee on ordained ministry in consultation with the DS. (See ¶¶314 and 349.1b, *Discipline*)

Resources for licensing school and Course of Study are found in the appendix and at the GBHEM Web site.

Section 4:
Continuing as a
Certified Candidate

Continuing Certified Candidacy: The Work of the Spirit

It is easy to be distracted by the challenges and responsibilities of being a student, a candidate, a family member, and church worker. Therefore, it is important to continue to set aside time to focus on your spiritual growth.

Attending to the Spirit

The following experiences are suggestions of ways to reflect with your mentor on the work of the Holy Spirit in your life, ministry, and relationships, especially as you continue to discern, reflect and make decisions regarding your future ministry in The United Methodist Church. Choose the ones that fit your needs and circumstances.

- Plan to attend worship in a setting different from your own home church to expose you to cultural and theological differences.
  - Note differences between worship as you have known it and this new experience. Look at the purpose of the worshipping community and how worship fulfilled that purpose.

  - If you are looking toward a specialized ministry, evaluate your worship experience in light of that specialization.

Choose to explore the situations and issues in this chapter that fit your circumstance, or adapt the questions to fit your circumstance.

The candidacy mentor is encouraged to be flexible and adjust the procedures and conversations to enable you to obtain maximum benefit.

- Spend a day accompanying a deacon, elder, or local pastor in ministry. Contact the person in advance to share what you want to do, and ask them if they are willing to share their lives with you in this way.
  - Note here some reflection questions that you can ask this deacon, elder, or local pastor about how she or he experiences the Spirit in her or his work setting.

  - After your time of accompanying, reflect with your candidacy mentor on the experience. What was most helpful to your decision-making process?

- Each time you meet with your candidacy mentor, discuss the following questions:
  - Where have you most recently seen God at work in your life?

○ What are the devotional practices that are currently sustaining you?

○ What spiritual practices have you developed that will be ongoing sources of spiritual nourishment to you wherever you are?

• It will be necessary for you to renew your spirituality daily in order to maintain your vision of licensed or ordained ministry. Read John 6:25-40.
  ○ What insights about spiritual renewal did you find in the passage from John?

  ○ How do you plan to keep in touch with the spiritual nourishment that comes from God, especially in times of greatest stress? Discuss and record here your plan for spiritual renewal with your candidacy mentor.

Continuing Certified Candidacy: The Process

If you are pursuing licensing as a local pastor, you will continue as a certified candidate with your candidacy mentor until you complete licensing school, are licensed as a local pastor, and are appointed as a local pastor. The license is awarded when you are appointed. You will then be enrolled in a prescribed Course of Study or be continuing your seminary studies. You will then be assigned a clergy mentor who will continue with you until you complete the Course of Study or your seminary studies. (¶316.4 *Discipline*)

If you are pursuing ordination as deacon or elder and you are not appointed as a licensed local pastor, your period as a certified candidate may continue from one to twelve years until you become a provisional member of an annual conference. During this time you will continue with your seminary studies and work with your candidacy mentor until you become a provisional member. (See page 159.)

In your studies toward licensed or ordained ministry, your failure to make satisfactory progress or to keep your dCOM informed of your progress may cause your candidacy to lapse. (¶312, *Discipline*)

Maintaining Contacts through Certified Candidacy

The following five parties are important contacts for you as you progress toward licensed or ordained ministry:

1) district superintendent
2) district committee on ordained ministry
3) charge conference, your appointed charge, or equivalent
4) candidacy mentor or clergy mentor
5) educational institution

It is important for the candidacy mentor and candidate for licensing as a local pastor to review the remainder of this section to see what studies might be needed before licensing.

District Superintendent

Your district superintendent participates through information-sharing, recommending, and pastoral care:

- As a member of the dCOM, to approve your year of service required during certified candidacy: "Each candidate shall have demonstrated his or her gifts for ministries of service and leadership to the satisfaction of the district committee on ordained ministry as a condition for provisional membership." (¶324.2)
- "to issue and renew licenses to preach when authorized (¶422.2)
- "to maintain regular communication with all candidates in order to advise and encourage them in spiritual and academic preparation for their ministry." (¶422.2)

District Committee on Ordained Ministry

The dCOM is the official body through which you and the church remain in contact concerning your continuing progress toward licensed or ordained ministry.

- Interview the candidate annually to continue candidacy when the following conditions are met satisfactorily: (¶312)
  - Candidate has received the annual recommendation of the charge conference or equivalent body;
  - Candidate is making satisfactory progress in studies, having presented an official transcript;
  - Candidate continues to evidence gifts, fruits and God's grace for the work of ministry.
- Offer counsel to candidates regarding pre-theological studies. (¶665.4)
- Maintain a service record and file of every local pastor and

candidate until the individual becomes an associate or provisional member. (¶665.7)

- Recommend to the board of ordained ministry those who qualify for associate and provisional membership. (¶665.8)
- Recommend to the board of ordained ministry those who qualify for license or continuance as local pastors. (¶665.8)
- A licensed local pastor who is completing the Course of Study may be asked to present annually to the district committee a report of satisfactory progress in prescribed courses.

You are encouraged to take initiative to maintain contact with your dCOM. Often your cooperation and initiative may be interpreted as one indicator of your interest in continuing in licensed or ordained ministry and the strength of your desire to fulfill the appropriate requirements in the candidacy process. Contact with your dCOM may be continued informally by letter, e-mail, telephone, or a personal visit to the chairperson of the committee or to your district superintendent.

Charge Conference or Equivalent; Appointed Charge as a Local Pastor

Your local church charge conference or equivalent body specified by the district committee on ordained ministry, or the charge to which you are appointed as a licensed local pastor, must annually recommend your renewal to the dCOM. (¶¶247.9 and 312) This is the opportunity for the church to re-examine its initial recommendation of you for candidacy in light of your subsequent growth and performance, or fruit, as a candidate or licensed local pastor.

To be considered for renewal, you will need to consult with the pastor or other persons as appropriate. You are expected to take initiative in this procedure and to make a brief report of your progress as requested.

Candidacy Mentor or Clergy Mentor as Licensed Local Pastor

It is important that you continue to be in regular contact with your mentor throughout your candidacy process and/or studies.

- It is expected that you will meet with that person at least twice each year. This contact will be part of the official relationship between you and your dCOM.
- An annual report on your vocational goals and progress toward

ordination or completion of Course of Study will be sent to the committee by your mentor.

Your mentor can continue to be valuable to you in planning and evaluating all facets of your progress as a licensed local pastor or toward ordained ministry. Any questions you may have about your progress can be discussed with your mentor in confidence.

Educational Institutions

To continue as a candidate or in the Course of Study you must make satisfactory progress in your educational studies. You should consult with the dCOM to obtain agreement on what will constitute satisfactory progress in these studies or in the process for ordained ministry.

Continuing Certified Candidacy: Continued Study

One of the ways to develop your skills and your potential for ordained ministry is through your educational preparation. Adequate educational preparation is expected of every licensed local pastor and clergy member of an annual conference.

The minimal educational requirement for **licensed local pastors** is a high school diploma or equivalent, licensing school, and the basic five-year prescribed Course of Study. (See appendix C or www.gbhem/ls-cos.)

For people pursuing **ordained ministry**, the Bachelor of Arts (or equivalent degree) is the norm. The Master of Divinity degree is the norm for ordained elder and a master's degree that is inclusive of or in addition to basic graduate theological studies (BGTS) is the norm for ordained deacons. All studies are to be from institutions recognized by the University Senate of The United Methodist Church.

In addition the *Book of Discipline*, ¶324, 5-6, outlines alternative methods of preparation for those persons seeking deacons orders who are at least 35 years of age, or those persons seeking elders orders who are at least 40 years of age. (See page 155.)

Certified Candidate Licensed as a Local Pastor

If you have discerned a call to pastoral ministry, you will need to be licensed for pastoral ministry following a period of prescribed education. You must first become a certified candidate; then complete the educational requirements for licensing; and receive an appointment.

> *A certified candidate is eligible for appointment as a licensed local pastor upon completion of License for Pastoral Ministry. (¶314, Discipline)*

Being eligible for appointment as a local pastor means that you will be appointed as need arises; there is no obligation of the annual conference to appoint local pastors to charges. The award of a license is not made until a person is actually appointed to a parish as its pastor.

The Process to become Licensed:

All persons not ordained as elders who are appointed to preach and conduct divine worship and perform the duties of a pastor shall have a license for pastoral ministry. The board of ordained ministry may recommend to the executive session of the annual conference the licensing of those persons who have completed the following: (¶315.2, 6, *Discipline*)

- *The conditions for candidacy certification in ¶¶311.1-2 (page 24 of this Guidebook) and;*
- *The studies for the license as a local pastor as prescribed and supervised by the Division of Ordained Ministry or one-third of their work for a Master of Divinity degree at a school of theology listed by the University Senate;*
- *Been examined and recommended by the district committee on ordained ministry.*

In every case, those who are licensed shall have:
- *Released the required psychological reports, criminal background and credit checks, and reports of sexual misconduct and/ or child abuses. They shall submit, on a form provided by the conference board of ordained ministry;*
  - *a notarized statement detailing any convictions for felony or misdemeanor or written accusations of sexual misconduct or child abuse; or*
  - *a notarized statement certifying that the candidate has not been convicted of a felony or misdemeanor, or accused in writing of sexual misconduct or child abuse.*

If you have discerned a call to pastoral ministry, you will need to be licensed as a local pastor.

Your **candidacy mentor** will help you understand and meet those requirements.

Once you are licensed as a local pastor and receive an appointment, you will work with a **clergy mentor** while in the Course of Study.

- *been approved by the board of ordained ministry;*
- *provided the board with a satisfactory certificate of good health on a prescribed form from a physician approved by that board.*

The studies for license as a local pastor are offered by the annual conference BOM according to guidelines developed by the Division of Ordained Ministry. The guidelines suggest a minimum total of 80 hours of study in four practical areas: Worship and Preaching, Church Administration, Christian Education, and Pastoral Care.

Students who have completed one third of the work required for an M.Div. degree may be approved for license as a local pastor without completing the licensing studies provided through the annual conference.

Following Licensing and Appointment:

A licensed local pastor is responsible to the district superintendent and to the clergy session of the annual conference in the performance of duties as a pastor. (¶316.4, 5, *Discipline*)

In addition, the dCOM must annually renew its recommendation of the person as a local pastor. This latter recommendation must be confirmed by the clergy session of the annual conference. (¶316.2 and ¶635.2g)

Those appointed as local pastors are clergy members of the annual conference and are no longer listed as certified candidates. They do not continue with candidacy mentors but are assigned a clergy mentor. (¶314 *Discipline*)

See www.gbhem.org/ls-cos) for information about licensing schools and the prescribed Course of Study for licensed local pastors.

Note your questions for your mentor here about requirements for license as a local pastor:

Course of Study for Local Pastors

If you are a candidate for license as a local pastor and are not enrolled in seminary, you will be required to enroll in the Course of Study.

What is it?

The Course of Study is a basic theological education program prescribed by the General Board of Higher Education and Minsitry, Division of Ordained Ministry. It is required for those who are licensed as local pastors and who are not attending an approved seminary. (See Appendix C and www.gbhem/ls-cos.)

Who Attends?

Participants in the program should have been approved as a certified candidate by the district committee for licensed or ordained ministry, completed the studies for license for pastoral ministry, and been recommended for licensing by the dCOM.

Where and When is it Available?

The Course of Study is offered at regional Course of Study schools each summer on the campuses of several United Methodist theological seminaries. Go to the GBHEM Web site (www.gbhem/ls-cos) to see the locations for Course of Study schools.

Most courses are offered in a two-week module that allows both full-time and part-time local pastors to attend. Many of the regional schools have extension centers for part-time local pastors only. Go to www.gbhem/ls-cos. These extension centers usually offer courses in a two- or three-weekend format which allows bivocational local pastors to participate without taking time away from their work or family. Students who are unable to attend any of these schools may, with the permission of the Board of Ordained Ministry, take their courses through the correspondence curriculum provided by the Division of Ordained Ministry. Go to www.gbhem/ls-cos.

See Appendix C for more details concerning the basic Course of Study. Information follows on page 155 regarding how licensed local pastors who complete the requirements of the basic Course of Study may continue their preparation for ordination as an elder through an Advanced Course of Study program.

Reflection with your Candidacy Mentor

Read through the material on Course of Study in Appendix C. What other questions or concerns do you have about preparing for licensed or ordained ministry through the Course of Study? Discuss them with your candidacy mentor.

Theological Education for Elders and Deacons
Educational Requirements

The general assumption is that candidates for ordained ministry will progress in their educational work through college and seminary and/or graduate education.

Review the educational requirements from the *Book of Discipline* that are printed here regarding educational preparation for ordained ministry, particularly the route you intend to follow.

Undergraduate Education

Theological study as accredited by the Association of Theological Schools (ATS) and recognized by the University Senate of The United Methodist Church presupposes an appropriate accredited bachelor's degree. Persons pursuing ordination must meet the following undergraduate requirement:

- *A candidate for probationary membership shall have completed a bachelor's degree from a college or university recognized by the University Senate. Exceptions to the undergraduate degree requirements may be made in consultation with the General Board of Higher Education and Ministry in some instances, for missional purposes, for persons who have a minimum of sixty (60) semester hours of Bachelor of Arts credit and:*
  - a) *have been prevented from pursuit of the normal course of baccalaureate education, or*
  - b) *are members of a group whose cultural practices and training enhance insight and skills for effective ministry not available through conventional formal education, or*
  - c) *have graduated with a Bachelor degree or its equivalent from a college notrecognized by the University Senate and have completed one half of the studies of the Master of Divinity or equivalent first professional degree in a school of theology listed by the University Senate.(¶324.3)*

The board of ordained ministry shall require an official transcript of credits from each school before recognizing any of the applicant's educational claims. In case of doubt, the board may submit a transcript to the General Board of Higher Education and Ministry. (¶324.7)

Graduate Theological Education

Persons pursuing ordination as deacon or elder must meet the

Choose to explore the situations and issues in this chapter that fit your circumstance or adapt the questions to fit your circumstance.

The candidacy mentor is encouraged to be flexible and adjust the procedures and conversations to enable you to obtain maximum benefit.

educational requirements through a graduate theological degree program at a school recognized by the University Senate of The United Methodist Church, which presupposes an appropriate accredited bachelor's degree.

- Candidates for deacon or elder shall have completed one-half of the basic graduate theological studies in the Christian faith (BGTS). These courses may be included within or in addition to a seminary degree. The BGTS must include courses in Old Testament; New Testament, theology; church history; mission of the church in the world; evangelism; worship/liturgy; and United Methodist doctrine, polity and history. (¶324.4)

  Basic graduate theological studies of the Christian faith willbe offered at several United Methodist seminaries in a variety of formats from short-term, intensive courses during the summer and January term, to one weekend a month during fall or spring term, to a weekly semester-long class. A comprehensive schedule of these courses may be viewed at the Web sites of the United Methodist seminaries. See www.gbhem.org/umseminaries.

- **A candidate for elder** shall have completed one-half of the studies toward a Master of Divinity degree or its equivalent, including one-half of the BGTS from a seminary listed by the University Senate.

- **A candidate for deacon** shall have:

  (1) completed one half of the studies of a master's degree from a United Methodist seminary or one listed by the University Senate; or

  (2) received a master's degree in the area of the specialized ministry in which the candidate will serve.

  If you have special gifts or interests for a particular type of ministry such as parish nursing, teaching, music, community organization, etc., you may have already completed a graduate degree in your area of specialization. That master's degree along with the required basicgraduate theological studies listed in (a) above will fulfill your educational requirements.

  (3) In each case, (1) and (2) above, the deacon candidate will have completed one half of the BGTS, in a context which will provide formation as a United Methodist deacon in full connection within a cohesive program developed by the seminary and approved

by the General Board of Higher Education and Ministry, documented by a record of completion from that school.

The board of ordained ministry shall require an official transcript of credits from each school before recognizing any of the applicant's educational claims. In case of doubt, the board may submit a transcript to the General Board of Higher Education and Ministry. (¶324.7)

Alternative Educational Option for Deacon Candidates over 35

Persons pursuing ordination as deacon in full connection have another educational option in addition to a graduate degree.

In some instances a candidate who is pursuing ordination to serve as deacon in full connection may fulfill the academic requirements through the following professional certification alternate route: (¶324.5)

- shall have reached thirty-five (35) years of age at the time to become a certified candidate;
- completed a bachelor's degree, received professional certification or license in the area of ministry in which the candidate will serve, have completed a minimum of eight semester hours of graduate credit or equivalent quarter hours in the area of specialization, and have been recommended by the conference board of ordained ministry.

    Areas of specialization might include Christian education, youth ministry, music ministry, counseling, church communications, church business administration, camp and retreat ministry, etc. To learn more about professional certification in The United Methodist Church go to www.gbhem.org/certification.

- have completed a minimum of twenty-four semester hours of the basic graduate theological studies at a school recognized by the University Senate.

Option for Local Pastors over 40 to Become Ordained Elders

Local pastors who complete the requirements of the Course of Study may continue their preparation for conference membership and ordination as an elder through an Advanced Course of Study program. The *Book of Discipline* requires that local pastors who seek ordination through advanced studies meet the following: (¶324.6)

- Reach forty (40) years of age;

- Satisfy all requirements of numbers 1-3 and 7-14 of ¶324.
- Complete the five-year Course of Study; and
- Complete an Advanced Course of Study consisting of thirty-two semester hours of graduate theological study or its equivalent as determined by the General Board of Higher Education and Ministry, including standard courses in United Methodist doctrine, polity, and history. These courses may be taken at an approved school of theology or through the independent study program of the Division of Ordained Ministry.

The policies of the Division of Ordained Ministry allow up to three courses from a regionally accredited graduate program to be applied to the Advanced Course of Study. Graduate transcripts must be sent to the Division of Ordained Ministry for evaluation before such credit may be granted.

Reflection with your mentor about your Education

Check with your candidacy mentor about any additional educational policies of your annual conference. List here any your annual conference requirements that go beyond the expectations of the *Book of Discipline*, and note questions.

If there are questions about your degree or the school you select, always check with your mentor or the candidacy registrar to be sure.

Ask about internship possibilities and how those hours count toward the requirements, required courses, service under the supervision of a district superintendent, and any other standards that would directly affect your educational preparation for ordained ministry.

With your mentor discuss your educational plan, its advantages and disadvantages.

Spend some time in prayer and discernment about the way your gifts can best be developed through your educational preparation.

Section 5:
Completing Candidacy

Preparing for Provisional Membership

You are entering a new venture in your spiritual journey as you complete your period of certified candidacy and seek to become a probationary member of the annual conference.

Reflect on your journey so far and your feelings as you enter this new phase of preparation for ordained ministry.

The *Book of Discipline* records the expectations for persons seeking provisional membership in ¶324. With your candidacy mentor, use the skills in prayer and discernment you have developed through the candidacy process as you work through these expectations one at a time to prepare for your interviews with the dCOM and with the annual conference BOM.

As you review these disciplinary requirements, note your questions to discuss with your candidacy mentor.

What do you most need to help you prepare for the commissioning interview?

Qualifications for Election to Provisional Membership

A person shall be eligible for election to provisional membership and commissioning in the annual conference by vote of the annual conference on recommendation of its board of ordained ministry after meeting the following qualifications.

1. **Candidacy Requirement:** Each candidate shall have been a certified candidate for provisional membership for at least one year and no more than twelve years.
2. **Service Requirement:** Each candidate shall have demonstrated his or her gifts for ministries of service and leadership to the satisfaction of the district committee on ordained ministry as a condition for provisional membership.
3. **Undergraduate Requirement:** A candidate for provisional membership shall have completed a bachelor's degree from a college or university recognized by the University Senate. Exceptions to the undergraduate degree requirements may be made in consultation with the General Board of Higher Education and Ministry in some instances, for missional purposes, for persons who have a minimum of sixty semester hours of Bachelor of Arts credit and:
   a) have been prevented from pursuit of the normal course of baccalaureate education,
   b) are members of a group whose cultural practices and train-

ing enhance insight and skills for effective ministry not available through conventional formal education, or

c) have graduated with a Bachelor degree or its equivalent from a college not recognized by the University Senate and have completed one half of the studies of the Master of Divinity or equivalent first professional degree in a school of theology listed by the University Senate.

4. **Graduate Requirement:**

a) Candidates for deacon or elder shall have completed one-half of the basic graduate theological studies (BGTS) in the Christian faith. These courses may be included within or in addition to a seminary degree. These basic graduate theological studies must include courses in: Old Testament; New Testament; theology; church history; mission of the church in the world; evangelism; worship/liturgy; and United Methodist doctrine, polity, and history.

b) a candidate for ordination as an elder shall have completed one-half of the studies toward a Master of Divinity degree or its equivalent, including one half of the basic graduate theological studies from a seminary listed by the University Senate.

c) a candidate for ordination as a deacon shall have:

(1) completed one half of the studies of a master's degree from a United Methodist seminary or one listed by the University Senate, or

(2) received a master's degree in the area of the specialized ministry in which the candidate will serve, and

(3) completed one-half of the basic graduate theological studies, in a context which will provide formation as a United Methodist deacon in full connection within a cohesive program developed by the seminary and approved by the General Board of Higher Education and Ministry, documented by a record of completion from that school.

5. See page 155 for alternative plan for deacons.

6. See page 155 for plan for local pastors to become elders.

7. The board of ordained ministry shall require an official transcript of credits from each school before recognizing any of the applicant's educational claims. In case of doubt, the board may submit a *transcript* to the General Board of Higher Education and Ministry.

8. Each candidate shall present a *satisfactory certificate of good health* by a physician on the prescribed form. Disabilities are not to be construed as unfavorable health factors when a person with disability is capable of meeting the professional standards and is able to render effective service as a provisional member.

9. Each candidate shall respond to a *written and oral doctrinal examination* administered by the conference board of ordained ministry. The examination shall cover the following:

   a) Describe your personal experience of God and the understanding of God you derive from biblical, theological, and historical sources.

   b) What is your understanding of evil as it exists in the world?

   c) What is your understanding of humanity, and the human need for divine grace?

   d) How do you interpret the statement: Jesus Christ is Lord?

   e) What is your conception of the activity of the Holy Spirit in personal faith, in the community of believers, and in responsible living in the world?

   f) What is your understanding of the kingdom of God; the Resurrection; eternal life?

   g) How do you intend to affirm, teach and apply Part II of the *Discipline* (Doctrinal Standards and Our Theological Task) in your work in the ministry to which you have been called?

   h) The United Methodist Church holds that the living core of the Christian faith was revealed in Scripture, illumined by tradition, vivified in personal experience, and confirmed by reason. What is your understanding of this theological position of the Church?

   i) Describe the nature and mission of the Church. What are its primary tasks today?

   j) Discuss your understanding of the primary characteristics of United Methodist polity.

   k) How do you perceive yourself, your gifts, your motives, your role, and your commitment as a probationary member and commissioned minister in The United Methodist Church?

   l) Describe your understanding of diakonia, the servant ministry of the church, and the servant ministry of the probationary member and commissioned minister.

   m) What is the meaning of ordination in the context of the general ministry of the Church?

n) Describe your understanding of an inclusive church and ministry.

o) You have agreed as a candidate for the sake of the mission of Jesus Christ in the world and the most effective witness of the gospel, and in consideration of their influence as ministers, to make a complete dedication of yourself to the highest ideals of the Christian life, and to this end agree to exercise responsible self-control by personal habits conducive to bodily health, mental and emotional maturity, integrity in all personal relationships, fidelity in marriage and celibacy in singleness, social responsibility, and growth in grace and the knowledge and love of God. What is your understanding of this agreement?

p) Explain the role and significance of the sacraments in the ministry to which you have been called.

10. Each candidate shall have been recommended in writing to the conference board of ordained ministry, based on a three-fourths majority vote of the district committee on ordained ministry.

11. Each candidate shall have a personal interview with the conference board of ordained ministry to complete his or her candidacy.

12. Each candidate shall submit on a form provided by the board of ordained ministry a notarized statement detailing any convictions for felony, or misdemeanor, or written accusations and its disposition of sexual misconduct or child abuse; or certifying that this candidate has not been convicted of a felony or misdemeanor or accused in writing of sexual misconduct or child abuse. The candidate also shall release required psychological reports, criminal background, credit checks and reports of child abuse.

13. Each candidate shall file with the board a written, concise, autobiographical statement (in duplicate on a prescribed form) regarding age, health, family status, Christian experience, call to ministry, educational record, formative Christian experiences, and plans for service in the Church.

14. Each candidate shall have been recommended in writing to the clergy session based on at least a two-thirds majority vote of the conference board of ordained ministry.

Commissioning

With your candidacy mentor, read and reflect on the statement about the meaning of commissioning from ¶325, the *Discipline*:

> *Commissioning is the act of the Church that publicly acknowledges God's call and the response, talents, gifts, and training of the candidate. The church invokes the Holy Spirit as the candidate is commissioned to be a faithful servant leader among the people, to lead the church in service, to proclaim the Word of God and to equip others for ministry.*
>
> *Through commissioning, the church sends persons in leadership and service in the name of Jesus Christ and marks their entrance into a time of provisional membership as they prepare for ordination. Commissioned ministers are clergy members of the annual conference in provisional membership and are accountable to the bishop and the clergy session for the conduct of their ministry.*
>
> *During provisional membership the clergy session discerns their fitness for ordination and their effectiveness in ministry. After fulfilling all candidacy requirements and upon recommendation of the conference board of ordained ministry, the clergy session shall vote on the provisional membership and commissioning of the candidates. The bishop and secretary of the conference shall provide credentials as a provisional member and a commissioned minister in the annual conference.*
>
> *The period of commissioned ministry is concluded when the provisional members are received as full members of the annual conference and ordained as either deacon or elder, or a decision is made not to proceed toward ordination and provisional membership is ended.*

As you move closer to the time when you will be recommended for provisional membership, check with your annual conference candidacy registrar about its process and requirements for completing candidacy and election to provisional membership.

In your own words, note here how you would tell someone what commissioning means.

If you were a member of the personal interview committee from the BOM, what questions would you want to ask a candidate for provisional membership? Note the questions here and share your responses with your candidacy mentor.

What questions would you like to ask the interview committee or board of ordained ministry about commissioning or provisional membership?

Service of Provisional Members

You will be expected to be in ministry during your probationary period. Read ¶326 from the *Book of Discipline* and discuss its meaning with your candidacy mentor.

All persons who are provisional members shall be appointed by a bishop (¶430) and serve as a provisional member of the annual conference for a minimum of two years following the completion of education requirements for full connection. During the provisional period, arrangements shall be offered by the board of ordained ministry for all provisional members to be involved in a residency curriculum that extends theological education by using covenant groups and mentoring to support the practice and work of their ministry as servant leaders, to contemplate the grounding of ordained ministry, and to understand covenant ministry in the life of the conference. Provisional members may be appointed to attend school, to serve as elders in extension ministry, or as deacons in appointments beyond the local church. Wherever they are appointed, the service of provisional members shall be evaluated by the district superintendent and the board of ordained ministry in terms of the provisional member's ability to express and give leadership in servant ministry.

1. **Provisional members planning to give their lives as deacons** *in full connection shall be in ministries of Word and Service in the local church or in an approved appointment beyond the local church. A provisional member preparing for ordination as a deacon shall be licensed for the practice of ministry during provisional membership to perform the duties of the ministry of the deacon as stated in ¶328 and be granted support as stated in ¶331.14.*

2. **Provisional members planning to give their lives as elders** *in full connection shall be in ministries of Word, Sacrament, Order, and Service in the local church or in an approved extension ministry. A provisional member preparing for ordination as an elder shall be licensed for pastoral ministry (¶315).*

3. **Provisional members who are serving in extension ministries,** *enrolled in graduate degree programs, or appointments beyond the local church shall be accountable to the district superintendent and the board of ordained ministry for the conduct of ministry, and for demonstrating their effectiveness in the ministry of the order to which they seek to be ordained. In all cases, they will also demonstrate their effectiveness in servant leadership in the local church to the satisfaction of the board of ordained ministry.*

4. Provisional members seeking to change their ordination track shall:
   a) *Write to the board of ordained ministry and inform the district superintendent and bishop of their intention.*
   b) *Interview with the board of ordained ministry to articulate and clarify their call.*
   c) *Fulfill academic and service requirements.*

Upon the recommendation of the board of ordained ministry and by vote of the clergy session the person may be received into full connection with the annual conference and be ordained into the order to which they are transitioning.

Discuss the expectations of the probationary period with your candidacy mentor. Note questions here that you want to ask the annual conference BOM.

Talk with your candidacy mentor about the way a probationary service appointment is made in your annual conference and how you might participate in the decision.

Have your candidacy mentor outline the process of examination by the annual conference BOM with you.

Talk about ways you might present yourself during the interview in order to reflect the process of discernment you have been through, your belief in the guidance of the Holy Spirit, and your own identity in ordained ministry.

Discuss the role of your candidacy mentor in this process. Make arrangements to meet with your candidacy mentor one more time after your interview with the BOM so that you may reflect on the process.

Continued Growth as a Provisional Member

Throughout your provisional period, you will continue to work on spiritual growth and ordained ministry skills with a clergy mentor. As you come to the end of your time with your candidacy mentor, use this unit as a way to celebrate your life together as you look ahead to service as a commissioned minister.

The orders

The orders are described in the *Book of Discipline*:

¶306. *Order of Deacons and Order of Elders*—There shall be in each annual conference an Order of Deacons and an Order of Elders. All persons ordained as clergy in The United Methodist Church upon election to full membership in the annual conference shall be members of and participate in an Order appropriate to their election. An order is a covenant community within the church to mutually support, care for, and hold accountable its members for the sake of the life and mission of the church. These orders, separately or together, seek to respond to the spiritual hunger among clergy for a fulfilling sense of vocation, for support among peers during this stressful time of change in the Church, and for a deepening relationship with God.

¶307. *Purpose of an Order*—The specific and limited function of each Order is to: (1) provide for regular gatherings of ordained deacons and ordained elders for continuing formation in relationship to Jesus Christ through such experiences as Bible study, study of issues facing the church and society, and theological exploration in vocational identity and leadership; (2) assist in plans for individual study and retreat experiences; (3) develop a bond of unity and common commitment to the mission and ministry of The United Methodist Church and the annual conference; (4) enable the creation of relationships that allow mutual support and trust; and (5) hold accountable all members of the Order in the fulfilling of these purposes. All of the functions of the Order(s) shall be fulfilled in cooperation and coordination with the board of ordained ministry and do not replace the normal supervisory processes, the processes of evaluation for ordained ministers, or the responsibilities of the board of ordained ministry, the cabinet, or the clergy session.

Reflection with your candidacy mentor

Talk with your candidacy mentor about your understanding of an order. What is it that you look forward to as being part of an order?

Note here questions you have about the orders for ordained ministry.

What contributions do you think you can make to the development of these orders in The United Methodist Church?

A developing tradition

Conversations about the nature and forms of ministry in The United Methodist Church have been ongoing across the history of the denomination. Diaconal ministry legislation was first passed by the General Conference in 1976. Since that time, our understandings of diaconal ministry have continued to take shape. From 1976 to 1996, there have been numerous studies of ministry on behalf of the church. These discussions continue reflection on the nature of ministry begun long ago with the disciples of Jesus. A summary of the history of ministry can be found in Appendix B in this *Candidacy Guidebook*.

You are part of this developing tradition. As you become part of the Order of Deacons or Order of Elders, you will be helping to shape a vision for ordained ministry for our time.

If you have not read the documents in Appendix B, read them now and list the questions or issues that you want to discuss with your candidacy mentor. What issues does ordained ministry face today that are similar to issues addressed in previous times?

As you have opportunity, talk with those who have been in your annual conference for a number of years about their understanding of ordained ministry and the work of the study committees on ministry. Find someone who has been a delegate to General Conference (usually listed in the conference journal) or worked on a ministry study committee and visit with them about their understanding of the developing tradition of ordained ministry in The United Methodist Church.

Talk with a retired minister about the changes he or she has seen in the developing understandings of licensed and ordained ministry.

What would you like to contribute to the developing tradition of ordained ministry?

How will you mentor and/or befriend those just coming into candidacy?

Professional relationships

You will be in a place of ordained ministry during your provisional period. Each ordained ministry setting involves professional relationships with others. With your candidacy mentor, reflect on the qualities you want to cultivate in these relationships.

Relationships with other clergy

What kind of relationships do you currently have with other United Methodist clergy? What kind do you hope to have?

How will you relate with clergy of other denominations?

How will you relate to clergy who give oversight to your ordained ministry?

Staff relationships

If you serve in a church or agency with one or more staff members, it will be important to think about the following:

Describe the kind of relationships you would like to have with the professional staff with whom you work.

How can you assess your relationships with support staff and find resources to help you understand and improve those relationships?

In what creative ways could personal and professional growth be enhanced for all persons on your staff?

Other professional relationships

Relationships with parishioners, clients, students, and others will also be part of your ordained ministry. Use this opportunity to reflect on past experience as a way to describe the kinds of professional relationships you would like to build in your ordained ministry.

Discuss any significant learning from your relationship with your candidacy mentor. How could this experience model ways you might learn from other relationships?

How would you define professional? What kinds of boundaries does this word imply? In what ways might those boundaries function as barriers?

What strategies do you have for maintaining professional relationships in order to guard against abuse of power, sexual misconduct, and other hazards of ordained ministry?

Goals and expectations

As you look ahead to your ordained ministry, reflect on your goals and expectations with your candidacy mentor.

How will you continue to discern God's call in your life?

How will you continue to grow spiritually, personally, professionally? How will you "go on to perfection"?

What strategies and resources for your continuing spiritual and other growth are you able to name at this time?

As you assess your situation, record the expectations you have about your place of ordained ministry, job description, time involvement, salary and benefits, etc.

Rights and responsibilities

With your commissioning come new rights and responsibilities recorded in the *Book of Discipline*. Review this legislation and any questions you may have with your candidacy mentor.

¶327. *Eligibility and Rights of Provisional Membership—Provisional members are on trial in preparation for membership in full connection in the annual conference as deacons or elders. They are on probation as to character, servant leadership, and effectiveness in ministry. The annual conference, through the clergy session, has jurisdiction over provisional members. Annually, the board of ordained ministry shall review and evaluate their relationship and make recommendation to the clergy members in full connection regarding their continuance. No member shall be continued in provisional membership beyond the eighth regular session following their admission to provisional membership and commissioning. Years during which provisional members are appointed to attend school or as a local pastor shall not be counted in these limits.*

1. *Provisional members who are preparing for deacon's or elder's orders may be ordained deacons or elders when they qualify for membership in full connection in the annual conference.*

2. *Provisional members shall have the right to vote in the annual conference on all matters except the following:*

   a) *constitutional amendments;*

   b) *all matters of ordination, character, and conference relations of clergy.*

When they have completed all of their educational requirements and have served a minimum of two years under appointment immediately prior to election, they shall have the right to vote on election of delegates to general, jurisdictional, or central conferences.

3. *Provisional members may serve on any board, commission, or committee of the annual conference except the board of ordained ministry (¶635.1). They shall not be eligible for election as delegates to the General, central, or jurisdictional conferences.*

4. *Provisional members shall be amenable to the annual conference in the performance of their ministry and are subject to the provisions of the* Book of Discipline *in the performance of their duties. They shall be supervised by the district superintendent under whom they are appointed. They shall also be assigned a deacon or elder as mentor by the board of ordained ministry. Provisional members preparing to become elders shall be eligible for appointment by meeting disciplinary provisions (¶315).*

5. *Provisional members in appointments beyond the local church shall relate*

themselves to the district superintendent in the area where their work is done. The district superintendent shall give them supervision and report annually to their board of ordained ministry.

God Be With You

Reflection with your candidacy mentor

What are the things you remember most out of your candidacy process?

Name the times of accomplishment and the times of struggle and how they became significant in the process.

Share what you value about each other.

Explore and be clear about expectations for any continuing relationship between you and your candidacy mentor.

Create a way for remembering the journey you have traveled together with your candidacy mentor such as selecting a hymn that reflects your time together, writing a prayer, or footwashing. Pray together for the journey ahead as both of you move into new relationships and new ventures in ordained ministry.

Section 6:
Resources

Annotated Bibliography

United Methodist resources

The 2008 Book of Discipline of the United Methodist Church. The *Discipline* provides the heritage and understanding of The United Methodist Church through foundational historical and theological statements, a statement of social principles which guide lives of discipleship, and polity structure and guidelines for The United Methodist Church.

The United Methodist Book of Worship © 1992. This book is the basic resource for worship in the United Methodist Church and reflects Anglican, Evangelical United Brethren, and Methodist heritage. Liturgies for worship and prayers for many occasions are included in this important resource.

The United Methodist Hymnal © 1989. From the beginning, Methodists have been known as "a singing people." This resource not only includes hymns from diverse ethnic sources, but also creeds, prayers, and services for Sunday worship, celebration of the sacraments, and other times of worship.

Candidacy program resources

The Christian as Minister continues to be a basic resource for persons inquiring about and exploring ministry. It is based on the understanding that through baptism we are all participants in Christ's ministry. It examines the meaning of servant ministry and servant leadership and outlines the steps into ordained ministry. The book, which helps persons explore all forms of ministry in The United Methodist Church including deacon, elder, local pastor, professional certification, chaplaincy, campus ministry, and mission service, may be ordered from Cokesbury at 1-800-672-1789 or www.cokesbury.com.

Understanding God's Call: A Ministry Inquiry Process guidebook is an informal inquiry into God's call to minister in the name of Jesus Christ, that is to be shared with a guide for the discernment process. It explores biblical and spiritual understandings of the call to ministry and the unique heritage of The United Methodist Church. Copies of the *Ministry Inquiry Process* may be purchased through Cokesbury.

Candidates who wish to explore ministry as a deacon, an elder, or a local pastor, should register with the Division of Ordained Ministry and receive the *Guidelines for Candidacy* to be used with a candidacy mentor. This edition is based on John Wesley's criteria for ministerial candidates: "Do they have the grace, gifts, and fruit." In the process, candidates clarify their call, prepare to publicly declare their call before the charge conference, and seek certification as a candidate for ministry as a deacon, elder, or local pastor.

Faith resources

Carder, Kenneth L. *Living Our Beliefs: The United Methodist Way.* Nashville: Discipleship Resources.

Felton, Gayle. *By Water and the Spirit: A Study of Baptism for United Methodists.* Nashville: General Board of Discipleship, 1993. Leader's guide and participant workbook for study of baptism.

Maddox, Randy L. *Responsible Grace: John Wesley's Practical Theology.* Nashville: Abingdon Press, 1994. This books examines what it means to do theological reflection from a Wesleyan perspective and how that reflection can inform the ministry of the church today.

Williams, Colin W. *John Wesley's Theology Today.* Nashville: Abingdon Press, 1972. Examines the primary beliefs of John Wesley in comparison to views of the other reformers.

Ministry resources

Balswick, Jack and Judith Balswick. *The Dual-Earner Marriage: The Elaborate Balancing Act.* Grand Rapids, Mich.: Fleming H. Revell Company, 1995. Examines many issues faced by couples with both spouses working.

Banks, Robert, ed. *Faith Goes to Work: Reflections from the Marketplace.* Bethesda, Md.: The Alban Institute Inc., 1991. Testimonies from persons who have discovered the connection between their faith and their work.

Crabtree, Davida Foy. *The Empowering Church: How One Congregation Supports Lay People's Ministries in the World.* Bethesda, Md.: The Alban Institute Inc., 1989. Describes the adventure of a congregation that decided to be as serious about sending people into the world as about gathering them out of it.

Diehl, William. *The Monday Connection: A Spirituality of Competence, Affirmation and Support in the Workplace*. San Francisco: HarperCollins Publishers, 1992. Explores five types of ministry in daily life: competency, presence, ethics, change, and values.

Fortune, Marie M. *Is Nothing Sacred? When Sex Invades the Pastoral Relationship*. San Francisco: Harper & Row, 1992. This book addresses the ethics of pastor-parishioner relationships.

González, Justo, ed. *Each in Our Own Tongue: A History of Hispanic United Methodism*. Nashville: Abingdon Press, 1991. Historical contributions of Hispanics to United Methodism.

Guillermo, Artemio R., ed. *Churches Aflame: Asian Americans and United Methodism*. Nashville: Abingdon Press, 1991. The rise of Asian churches and their contribution to United Methodism.

Hartley, Ben L. and Paul E. Van Buren, *The Deacon: Ministry Through Words of Faith and Acts of Love*. Nashville: Section of Deacons and Diaconal Ministries, General Board of Higher Education and Ministry, 2000.

Law, Eric H.F. *The Wolf Shall Dwell with the Lamb: A Spirituality of Leadership in a Multicultural Community*. St. Louis, Mo.: Chalice Press, 1993. Raises awarenessof how ethnicity influenced leadership and what is needed to provide leadership in a multicultural society.

Malony, H. Newton, and Richard A. Hunt. *The Psychology of Clergy*. Harrisburg, Pa.: Morehouse Publishing Co., 1991. A guide to considering many dimensions of professional ministry, such as calling, use of time, family, dual careers, clergy couples, staff relationships, and effectiveness.

Menking, Stanley J., and Barbara Wendland. *God's Partners: Lay Christians at Work*. Valley Forge, Pa.: Judson Press, 1993. This book addresses how God is calling lay persons in the places where they live to do God's work in the world.

Noley, Homer. *First White Frost: Native Americans and United Methodism*. Nashville: Abingdon Press, 1991. The history of the Methodist attempt to evangelize Native Americans.

Osborn, Ronald E. *Creative Disarray: Models of Ministry in a Changing America*. St. Louis, Mo.: Chalice Press, 1992. Twelve classical models of ministry that have been shaped by religious life in the United States are examined with criteria for evaluating models of ministry.

Pierce, Gregory F., ed. *Of Human Hands: A Reader in the Spirituality of Work*. Minneapolis: Augsburg Fortress Publishers, 1991. Moving testimonies by persons in many walks of life who feel called by God to what they're doing all week long.

Roth, Bob. *Answering God's Call for Your Life*. Nashville: Division of Diaconal Ministry, General Board of Higher Education and Ministry, 2006. This book looks at Christian calls and church occupations and is focused for a youth and young adult audience.

Shockley, Grant S., ed. *Heritage and Hope: The African American Presence in United Methodism*. Nashville: Abingdon Press, 1991. The story of how the witness of African Americans contributed to United Methodist heritage.

Steinke, Peter L. *How Your Church Family Works: Understanding Congregations as Emotional Systems*. Bethesda, Md.: The Alban Institute Inc., 1993. A clear exposition of the congregation as a family system and a description of healthy leadership.

Swetland, Kenneth L. *The Hidden World of the Pastor*. Grand Rapids, Mich.: Baker Books, 1995. Provides thirteen cases, each illustrating a major issue that ordained persons face. A teaching guide suggests ways to use the case study method in supervision and professional education.

Wilke, Richard B. *Signs and Wonders: The Mighty Work of God in the Church*. Nashville: Abingdon Press, 1989. Examines God's actions in and through the church and challenges Christians to join in this rebirth.

Retreat resources

Job, Rueben. *A Journey to Solitude and Community*. Nashville: Upper Room Books, 1989. A guided retreat on spiritual formation with participant workbook.

Job, Rueben and Norman Shawchuck. *A Guide to Prayer*. Nashville: Upper Room Books, 1988. Includes weekly devotional themes and monthly retreat models.

Leech, Kenneth. *The Eye of the Storm: Living Spiritually in the Real World.* San Francisco: HarperCollins Publishers, 1992. Living spiritually in the real world . . . an excellent integration of the concern for spirituality and for social justice.

Smith, James Bryan. *A Spiritual Formation Workbook: Small Group Resources for Nurturing Christian Growth.* San Francisco: HarperCollins Publishers, 1993. Explores contemplative, holiness, charismatic, social justice, and evangelical traditions for spiritual growth.

Spiritual resources

Bondi, Roberta C. *In Ordinary Time: Healing the Wounds of the Heart.* Nashville: Abingdon Press. This book looks deeply at prayers through a series of letters to a younger friend.

Bondi, Roberta C. *Memories of God: Theological Reflection on a Life.* Nashville: Abingdon Press, 1995. In this book, Bondi relates everyday life to major theological concepts by describing how she came to understand them.

Hawkins, Thomas R. *Claiming God's Promises: A Guide to Discovering Your Spiritual Gifts.* Nashville: Abingdon Press, 1992. This book is about knowing what gifts from God one has and about using them.

May, Gerald. *The Awakened Heart: Living Beyond Addiction.* San Francisco: HarperCollins Publishers, 1991. Discusses how the invitation of love calls forth and develops the interior life.

McGinnis, James. *Journey into Compassion: A Spirituality for the Long Haul.* New York: Orbis Books, 1993. Explores lives of figures of compassionate commitment plus the practical steps of prayer and fasting for peacemaking and reconciliation.

Millard, Kent. *Get Acquainted with Your Christian Faith*, Leader's Guide and Study Book. Nashville: Abingdon Press. A workbook addressing how God creates, empowers, and calls us.

Miller, Wendy. *Learning to Listen: A Guide for Spiritual Friends.* Nashville: Upper Room Books, 1993. This book deals with the listening process especially as it relates to listening to God.

Palmer, Parker J. *The Active Life: A Spirituality of Work, Creativity, and*

Caring. San Francisco: HarperCollins Publishers, 1990. Addresses spirituality and spiritual practices for people who live a busy life.

Thompson, Marjorie J. *Soul Feast: An Invitation to the Christian Spiritual Life.* Louisville: The Westminster Press/John Knox Press, 1995. Offers spiritual practices and rule of life as a way to create space where God can nurture us.

Wuellner, Flora Slosson. *Prayer, Fear, and Our Power: Finding Our Healing, Release, and Growth in Christ.* Nashville: Abingdon Press, 1989. Many helpful exercises for dealing with fears and opening one's self more to God's power.

Yoder, John. *The Politics of Jesus: Vicit Agnus Naster.* Grand Rapids, Mich.: Eerdmans Publishing Co., 1994. Addresses teachings and ministry of Jesus as a guide to Christian behavior.

Appendix A

Models of Spiritual Discernment

Christians through the ages have wanted to do the will of God. The process of trying to discover what God wants or values is called **discernment**. You are trying to listen to God so as to know God's will.

Another definition of discernment is to see as God sees. In 1 Samuel 16, the great prophet Samuel goes at God's command to anoint a new king of Israel. Samuel knows that the new king is one of Jesse's sons. The sons come before Samuel one by one starting with the oldest. When Samuel sees the oldest son, Eliab, he thinks that surely this son is the one. But God says to Samuel, "Do not look on his appearance or on the height of his stature, because I have rejected him; for the Lord does not see as mortals see; they look on the outward appearance, but the Lord looks on the heart." (1 Samuel 16:7)

What you are really to be about as you move through these candidacy studies is learning to see more as God sees, especially regarding who you are, what gifts you have been given, the needs of the world, the needs of the mission of Christ in the world and in the church, and how God dreams you can best be a part of God's work in the world.

So discernment is both a state and a process. In discerning the ministry into which you are called on behalf of Christ, there are specific things that you or you and others can do to help you listen to what God wants. That process involves doing things that help you listen to God, sense God's direction, see what God sees.

There are three preconditions to discernment:

The first is to have a relationship to God as we know God through the life, ministry, death, and resurrection of Jesus Christ as that is manifested in Scripture, tradition, experience, and reason, and as revealed through the activity of the Holy Spirit to and in you. This first precondition means that you know God to be a loving God, who earnestly wants to be in communication with you. As a part of getting to know and to trust God, you discover ways of receiving that communication, of hearing God's voice, of seeing from Christ's perspective, of sensing the loving, healing presence of the Holy Spirit. One of the important skills needed for discernment is the *ability to receive that communication from God.*

The second precondition is wanting to know God's will. It is possible to relate to God without wanting to know what it is that God wants. It is also important to be sure that you are listening to God and not to other voices.

After his baptism, Jesus went into the wilderness to seek God's will. He went off by himself into the desert perhaps thinking he could hear God better there. He wanted to know that what he was hearing was from God. In this story of Jesus' temptations in the wilderness, it is very clear that some of the voices that Jesus heard were not God's voice. But for Jesus it had to be God's will.

Christians who practice discernment talk about a concept called "holy indifference." Holy indifference means that we want to know God's will badly enough that we are willing to lay aside any biases or desires that we have so that we may really hear God. Coming to holy indifference may well be the hardest part of the whole process since it means that you have come to the point of wanting God's will more than you want your own.

The third precondition for discernment is committing yourself to doing what you discern God wants. Sometimes there still must be a wrestling inside yourself that must occur, especially if the answer seems not to be the one for which you had been hoping. As an example, it is clear in the temptation story that Jesus became committed to doing what he heard from God, that is, to living his life and doing his ministry the way he discerned God wanted. But he had to struggle within himself with opposing tendencies; otherwise, the temptations would not have been temptations.

Once you have discerned what you believe to be God's will, you must hold it by faith. You can't be absolutely sure. However, there are some checkpoints that you can use.

- God's will is consistent with the major thrusts of Scripture.
- Often there will be an element of surprise involved.
- Check out what you have come to understand about God's will for you with a spiritually mature Christian whom you trust by asking if in their judgment what you have heard could be the will of God.
- If it is God's will, usually a sense of peace will come, and this sense of peace continues to feel right over time.

Here are six models for discernment that might be helpful to you. The first two are for personal discernment. The others are for discernment by groups.

Models of Personal Discernment

Model 1: Morris model

This model is taken from *Yearning to Know God's Will* by Danny Morris.

Preconditions

1. A desire to do God's will.
2. An openness to God.
3. An awareness of how God acts in order to recognize God's action.

Process

4. Use conventional methods to choose the best possibility.
5. Ask if this choice is God's will. This question needs to be a "yes" or "no" question, no multiple choice. Then wait patiently for the answer.
6. Consolation (peace, freedom, joy, lightness) or desolation (stifled, not right, uneasiness, anxiety) will come. Over time one of the two will prevail.

Model 2: Gestation

by Susan Ruach

1. Have holy intention of wanting what God wants.
2. Let the question rise up from within your depths, that is, be planted in yourself by God. After all, you have to have a question before you can have an answer.
3. Live with the question. Talk about it, rest with it, read with it in mind, work with it.
4. Always be listening.
5. Begin to see form, changing shape to the question. Be aware of kicks, nudges, movement.
6. At some moment you will come to an understanding. It will come to birth in God's own time.

Models for Corporate Discernment

Model 1. Discernment steps: Toward a vision of God's will

by Bishop David J. Lawson

1. One needs good data, basic factual information, identification of alternatives and possibilities.
2. Insist that all categories be kept soft in order that playfulness and creativity may be present and contribute to the process.
3. Maintain holy indifference to the outcome; lay aside all biases, prejudices; be willing to leave the outcome to God's direction and be obedient to the results.
4. Maintain a community and climate of worship.
5. Ask and respond to: Where have you sensed God's benediction in what we have been about?
6. Spend time in reflection, perhaps with a Scripture passage, seeking to listen to God's intimations in the future, hints of God's direction.
7. Share with the faith community what you have heard/seen/felt in your reflection time. Dialogue about what has been reported. Avoid debating for there is no right or wrong, win or lose, but rather a desire to listen to God. Frequently, insight and wisdom come in the dialogical space with a group.
8. Humility is crucial. Each one must be constantly aware that God may have spoken the definitive word to another person.
9. Sometimes silence is how the Christian community moves ahead.
10. Pause from time to time and ask: "God, are you trying to say anything to us? Are we missing anything here?"
11. Remember holy (sacred) indifference to the outcome. Be willing to receive wisdom or direction even if it does not fit your strong desires or decisions.
12. When agreement is reached, directions, plans, commitments are all offered to God. Sometimes the question: "Are we ready to offer this to God?" is helpful.

Model 2. Fenhagen Model

(from James C. Fenhagen, *Ministry and Solitude*. New York: The Seabury Press, 1981)

Next comes the process of deliberation. When a concern is brought to the surface and agreed upon as important enough to warrant such commitment, all possible evidence is gathered and made available to all who will be engaged in the deliberation. Then the process begins. In brief, it includes the following steps.

1. A period of meditation and prayer seeking openness to and guidance from the Spirit.
2. The sharing of "cons," as each person reports the reasons against moving in a particular direction that he personally discerns.
3. A period of prayer allowing time to reflect on the seriousness of the "cons" that have been shared.
4. A sharing of "pros," as each person reports his own personal discernment. If no consensus emerges, the process continues.
5. A period of prayer allowing time for reflection upon step 4.
6. An effort to sort out and weigh the reasons behind the pros and cons, recording those reasons so that they are available to all, and to discern communally, in the light of what has been listed, the choices to which the community is called by God. In commenting on this aspect of the process, Father Futrell writes, "If the Holy Spirit is working through the second time of election, and if the conditions of authentic communal discernment have been fulfilled (i.e., if there is genuine openness to the Spirit), the decision should be made clear, and confirmation should be experienced unanimously through shared deep peace . . . finding God together." (John Futrell, S. J. "Communal Discernment: Reflections on Experience," *Studies in the Spirituality of the Jesuits* IV, no. 5 [November 1972]: 173.)
7. A concluding prayer of thanksgiving and the reaffirmation of corporate commitment to carrying out the decision.

At first glance, such a process seems unduly long for the everyday decisions that take place within the life of a parish. That would depend, of course, on the time given to each step.

Group Model for Discernment in a Retreat Setting

What follows is a group model which could be used in a retreat setting as an optional model for candidacy mentors and several candidates focused on a particular section in the *Guidelines for Candidacy*. A retreat or other group model may be used, as long as the importance of time between sessions for reflection and assimilation is recognized.

Between retreat sessions, candidates may complete assigned tasks such as journaling or interviewing, do advance preparation for the next retreat session, and/or meet individually with a candidacy mentor. Please note that this retreat model is not to be a substitute for the candidate's relationship to a candidacy mentor which is at the heart of the candidacy process.

First Session
Friday evening
- Evening meal
- Opening worship
- Introductions
- "Sharing your faith story" (an opportunity for retreat participants to share their spiritual journeys)
- Bible study (of one biblical call)
- Evening silence until breakfast (time for individual reflection and journaling before bed)

Saturday morning
- Morning prayer
- Breakfast
- Session from "Exploring Your Call to Ordained Ministry" in the *Guidelines for Candidacy*
- Individual reflection time (for being outdoors, journaling, meeting with candidacy mentor)

Saturday afternoon
- Lunch
- Session from "Exploring Your Call to Ordained Ministry" in the *Guidelines for Candidacy*
- Break
- Group sharing/reflecting
- Planning ahead (what needs to be done before the next retreat, scheduling individual appointments, etc.
- Closing worship
- Adjourn

Two or three months may be needed between retreat sessions so that candidates can complete work in the *Guidelines for Candidacy*.

Second Session

The second retreat could deal with additional material from "Exploring Your Call to Ordained Ministry" in the *Guidelines for Candidacy*.

Third Session

A third retreat could deal with the decision-making process at the end of the section on "Exploring Your Call to Ordained Ministry" in the *Guidelines for Candidacy* followed by an individual meeting with a candidacy mentor to reflect on a decision, to provide closure, or to prepare for declaring candidacy. Plan time for celebration through individual and group affirmation.

Appendix B

History of the Deacon and Elder

"The words deacon, deaconess, and diaconate, all spring from a common Greek root—*diakonos*, or 'servant,' and *diakonia*, or 'service.'" (*Discipline*, ¶310). The diaconate in The United Methodist Church has its roots in early church tradition. The following is printed with the approval of the Permanent Diaconate Office, Diocese of Buffalo.

First century—There is very little evidence in the New Testament about the ordering of ministry. The term "ministry" denotes the service to which all people of God are called. Through the years the church has made a distinction between the call to all Christians to serve in the ministry of the laity and the call to servant leadership through ordained ministry. Tradition has, most frequently, associated the beginning of the diaconate with Acts 6:1-6 (C.E. 60-80) where the selection of seven men to serve in specific ways suggests a particular organization of church life in order to facilitate the work to be done.

The diaconate has a biblical heritage of service to the world and a history that has constantly been reshaped. Consequently, the understanding of the deacon's role, duties, and/or functions should be in response to the needs of the world and seen in light of the relationship with the community of believers which has verified her or his call.

The diaconate has existed since the first Christian communities. We find it in the communities founded by Paul at Philippi and at Ephesus (Philippians 1:1; 1 Timothy 3:8-12) about 50-60 C.E. Later, at the end of the first century, we find deacons referred to in the eastern church of Syria and by the Palestinian author of the *Didache** as well as in the western church of Corinth and Rome. At the time of the *Didache*, the deacons were elected by the people as were the bishops.

At this time, the work of deacons was already bound to the Eucharist. "On the Lord's Day, they assisted at the breaking of bread." The ministry of deacons was not confined only to the breaking of bread. According to the *Didache*, their ministry was identical to that of the prophets and teachers: they had the task of instructing and building up the church. The deacons did, by reason of their office, what the prophets and teachers accomplished as a result of a charism received from the Holy Spirit.

---

*Didache. The oldest known document of a class denoted as "Church Orders," compiled from various sources, containing directives for catechetical instruction, worship, and ministry (The Interpreters Dictionary of the Bible, Nashville: Abingdon Press, 1962).

Second century—In the second century, Ignatius of Antioch described a triple ministry consisting of bishops, priests, and deacons. The faithful had to obey deacons, as well as bishops and priests, and if they did something without them, "their conscience ought not to have been at peace." On the other hand, deacons had to submit to priests as well as bishops. Basically, they were to help the bishops; they were to render service in several ways:

a. The deacons wrote letters for the bishop; they strengthened and helped him in all his duties; they also helped him in the ministry of the Word of God.

b. Deacons were legates or messengers, and in that capacity they were God's ambassadors from one church to another, for example, on the occasion of a ceremony to celebrate peace after a persecution.

Ignatius did not mention that deacons should take care of widows, orphans, and the needy. It was enough for him to remind the deacons that they were not deacons to serve food and drink, but that they were ministers of God's church.

If the deacons took care of the poor and needy in the second century, they did not do it as a duty proper to their office, but as assistants to the bishop. To help the poor, to collect alms for widows, orphans, and needy persons, was above all the duty of the bishops as Justin and Hermas testified, or of the priests who, according to Polycarpe, should neglect not one widow, poor person, or orphan. According to the Apostolic Tradition of Hippolytus (third century), "it ought not to be the deacons, but the bishops who should visit the sick." The deacon was only to indicate to the bishop those who were sick in the community, "for the sick person is more comforted by the high priest rather than the deacon who remembered him."

It is important to recall that charitable works and aid to the poor and unfortunate was the proper function of the bishops alone and that the deacons only took part in it as their assistants. This practice of the second century is reflected in a description of the function of the diaconate as we see it in the Apostolic Tradition:

> *The deacon is not ordained with the priesthood in view, but for the ministry of the bishop according to what the latter may demand of him; he has no part in the presbyterate, but he takes care of the work designated by the bishop as being necessary to the church's ministry.*

We might say in modern terms that the deacon seems to be somewhat like a "specialist," assigned by the bishop to a designated area.

Third century—According to Cyril of Alexandria, the duty of deacons consisted of spiritual interpretation: "they taught and fulfilled what the Lord said and did."

Tertullian named the deacon among the ministers of baptism, and according to Saint Cyprian, in the absence of priests, the apostates who had received letters from martyrs could confess their faults to deacons who examined the conditions of their re-admission to the church. Besides, if there were no priest for a dying sinner, the deacon could hear his confession and lay hands on him before he presented himself before the Lord.

In this practice of reconciliation of sinners, the deacon seemed to act as the bishop's aide. Reconciliation of the sinner was a public action in which the deacon and the bishop participated as witnesses. In an emergency, however, the deacon, delegated by the bishop, acted as sole witness.

The Apostolic Tradition emphasized the fact that deacons did not receive the Spirit in the same way as priests, but they received the Spirit in order to be rendered fit to accomplish the work that the bishop wished to entrust to them. That is why only the bishop will impose his hands on the deacon. In the prayer for the ordination of deacons in this tradition, the bishop asks God to "grant the spirit of grace, application, and zeal to the servant that God has chosen to be a minister in God's church."

The service that deacons had to render to the bishop, according to the Apostolic Tradition, consisted in bringing the offering to the celebrant and assisting priests or bishops at baptism by carrying the oil of Thanksgiving and the oil of exorcism. At the Lord's Supper, they carried the lamp (Lucernarium), the symbol of Christ, and they recited the Alleluia verse.

According to the **Pseudo-Clementine**, the deacon "was the eye of the bishop;" the deacon had to observe what the members of the church were doing, especially those who were in danger of committing sin. The bishop had to have as many deacons as necessary to know all the members of the church and strengthen them through the deacons. We can say, therefore, that the ministry to which the deacons were ordained was a very specific ministry chosen by the bishop, and it was because of this ministry that the deacons were included in the clergy. The deacon is a minister because the deacon is a minister of the bishop.

It is important to remember that during the first centuries, the priests were never called ministers or assistants to the bishop. It was only from the third century that the distinction between bishops and priests was fixed unequivocally and the priest began to be called the bishop's auxiliary. From that time on in some manner, priests (no longer on the same level as the bishop) took the place of deacons.

Since they were priests, they seemed to be better assistants to the bishops than deacons, and the latter became less necessary. Thus, after an indispensable service of three centuries, the diaconate began to decline and to become a relic of the past without specific function. The reason for the disappearance of the permanent diaconate was the creation of a new form of the diaconate ministry in the third century, i.e. the priests. Priests could help the bishop not only in a specific ministry as did the deacons, but also could celebrate the Eucharist and administer the sacraments.

Thus we can see that the restoration of a diaconate in a new situation will not be able to succeed if it does not include a new creation of the diaconate with clearly defined functions alongside those of bishops and priests. A church that was able to designate the functions of priests as new assistants to the bishop in the bishop's ministry of service and liturgy could again create deacons in accord with the demand of the present situation.

Fourth century—In the fourth century, open polemics between priests and deacons appeared. While the priests tried to demonstrate that their function was the same as that of the bishops, the deacons applied themselves to proving their function was the same as that of the priests.

In several places, the deacons celebrated the Eucharist. The Council of Arles (A.D. 314) prohibited the deacons from doing this. A similar prohibition was given at the Council of Nicea. The Council of Ancyre (A.D. 314) even forbade deacons to preach. Jerome, who, as a priest, defended the equality of the priest and the bishop at the beginning of the church, also demonstrated the great difference between deacons and priests by saying that the diaconate had become a source of profit and the deacons had such material wealth that they stirred up envy among priests.

In this struggle for their identity, the deacons, especially in the Latin Rite, lost their spirit of service. They tried to demonstrate to themselves and others that they were still important and necessary because of their closeness to the bishop. This was not too difficult to establish. Being assistants to the bishop, they had certain means of which priests were completely deprived. As deacons, they were able to have more power and influence than the priests. As official inspectors, money collectors, counselors, and emissaries of the bishop, they had a knowledge of the affairs of the church that made them the best candidates for the episcopacy. In fact, they often succeeded their deceased bishop. This was frequently the case of the Archdeacon of Rome who, close to the Pope, was able to exercise a power not only over the priests but also over the rural bishops. It was not uncommon to have the Archdeacon ordained as bishop of Rome without first being ordained a priest.

The internal crisis of the diaconate, which began in the fourth century, did not immediately manifest itself throughout the entire church. Several centuries were necessary before the diaconate totally lost its *raison d' etre*. In many places, it continued to grow and flourish for a long time where its functions had been especially delineated by the bishop and deacons were supported and encouraged by the priests and lay people. During the fourth century, deacons still accompanied the bishops who visited the churches scattered throughout the countryside. Sometimes, they were sent alone to make the visit. They carried episcopal letters; they were present at synods with the bishops; and they frequently acted as delegates or representatives of sick bishops who could not be present at Councils. They were also an integral part of the tribunals with bishops and priests to arbitrate quarrels among Christians. During the liturgy, they led the prayers for the intentions of the church and the world.

The deacon also read the Psalms or the gospel during the Eucharistic celebration and pronounced publicly the names of those for whom Mass was being offered, as well as the intention of the prayers. During the office, the deacon gave certain instructions to the assembly of the faithful and it was up to the deacon to indicate to the catechumens when to withdraw. The deacon also had to seat the faithful, to keep order, to keep watch at the door. When the moment came for the Eucharistic oblation, the deacon had to stay near the bishop in order to help. The deacon also carried the water for the absolutions to the altar and gave communion to the people, but not to priests.

Deacons had to be well prepared to express themselves. In certain places, the deacon had to teach catechism. It was for a deacon that Saint Augustine wrote a catechism for the illiterate as a manual for deacons.

Beginning in the fourth century, we find conciliar documents forbidding deacons to marry. If, at the moment of their ordination, they were not married, they had to express their intention of eventually marrying to the bishop; otherwise, they were to be celibate and, if later they decided to marry, they were suspended from the ministry.

The confrontation between the diaconate and the priesthood made reflection on the characteristics proper to the diaconate in contrast with the priesthood and episcopacy necessary. A metaphor offers a comparison: while priests took care of the internal life of the church, deacons were like pioneers or frontiersmen. They went in search of those who were not yet in the church and they led them there. They had to exhort them to surrender to the church where they would be purified by the preaching of the priests and the bishop. Deacons had to be like Apostles, searching for persons in order to bring them into the church where the bishop, assisted by the priests, would nourish them, educate them and form Christ in them. The deacons thus became the missionaries of the bishop.

The function of the deacon as pioneer has received other explanations. The deacon is the one who brings the people toward God and takes away all obstacles. The priest continued this work by enlightening persons through the knowledge of God. The bishop consummated this activity by bringing the knowledge of the Trinity. This introductory role of deacons was also symbolized in the gesture of the deacon who accompanied to baptism the one who was to receive that sacrament. This introductory function was rapidly transferred to the order of the diaconate itself which was soon regarded as an introduction and a step toward the priesthood.

Fifth century—It seems that in the fifth century there were still churches where the deacons had all the powers including that of "breaking the bread" in the absence of priests. The charitable works of deacons become more and more vague. The protection and the care of the poor, originally entrusted to deacons, took on institutionalized form under the direction of the priests, religious, and laity. Certain deacons became simply responsible for the goods of the church. They were administrators of ecclesiastical possessions. But the majority of deacons gave themselves to the liturgy and the sacred chant. The church reproved deacons who devoted themselves only to the chant and did nothing for the poor.

Sixth century—In the sixth century, deacons were connected to cathedrals; they lived like canons. Deacons became more and more bound to the altar, chanting vespers and reciting the Psalms day and night. They succeeded in rendering themselves indispensable to the celebration of the Mass. A priest could not do by himself what the deacon had to do; for example, the priest could not take the chalice from the altar if the deacon did not give it to the priest. In the eighth century, Gregory I deplored the fact "that deacons were now ordained only to sing, and the first condition to be admitted to the diaconate was to have a beautiful voice, formerly they were ordained to preach and distribute alms."

Eleventh-sixteenth centuries—The permanent diaconate no longer existed in the Latin church. It was only a step toward the priesthood. The deacon had to teach, preach, and help the priest in the administration of the sacraments. The difference between the preaching of the deacon and that of the priest, according to Petrus Cantor, was that the deacon could not preach with authority like the priest.

The Council of Trent in the sixteen century declared that the hierarchy of bishops, priests, and deacons was of divine ordination. The restoration of the permanent diaconate was discussed at the council, but it was not acted upon.

With the coming of the reformers, Luther, Calvin, and Zwingli, to a church that was by that time so ensnared in hierarchy that it was captive to its own structure, the role of priest, deacon, and bishop drastically changed.

Various Protestant bodies retained, modified, or eliminated the concept of the diaconate. Where it was retained, its varied forms ranged from an order of clergy to an elected or appointed lay office. The Anglican Church retained the deacon as a probationary order of clergy or "stepping stone" to the priesthood—as in the Roman Catholic tradition. John Wesley, as an Anglican priest, brought that church's understanding of order to Methodism. However, the British Methodist Church, an outgrowth of Wesley's "societies," has never had a "stepping-stone" deacon. When Methodism was transplanted to America and Asbury was consecrated as the first bishop (in conflict with Wesley's wish that such functionaries be called "general superintendents"), he was ordained a deacon one day, an elder the following day, and made a bishop on the third day.

Thus the diaconate moved from an appointment by the church to a role of humble service to an established probationary order with rank and status, at times and in some traditions very powerful in church polity and structure. At other times and in some traditions, the deacon was reduced to an "inferior office," little more than a title, or cast aside altogether.

The diaconate has a biblical heritage of service to the world and a history which has constantly been reshaped. Consequently, the understanding of the deacon's role, duties, and functions of service should be in response to the needs of the world and seen in light of the relationship with the community of believers which has verified her or his call.

In 1964, Pope John XXIII began the restoration of the permanent diaconate within the Roman Catholic Church as suggested by the Second Vatican Council. Permanent deacons in the Roman Catholic Church are ordained to ministries of liturgy, word, and charity.

The Episcopal Church restored the order of permanent deacon in 1972, ordaining deacons to ministries of liturgy and service.

The Ministry of the Diaconate in Methodism

In The United Methodist Church, the office of deacon began with the deaconess movement. It is possible that the office of deacon in the early church was open to women. Phoebe is mentioned in the New Testament as a *diakonos* (deacon) and following in her footsteps women have served in specified forms of ministry ever since.

The Deaconess

The ministry of the deaconess in the free church tradition, such as the Methodist Church in the United States, can be understood only to the extent that one becomes acquainted with the background from which it has emerged historically and culturally.

The deaconess movement in American Methodism emerged during the latter part of the 19th century with the church's recognition of the increasing social problems confronting people, especially women and children, who were a part of a rapidly growing and expanding nation. These conditions aroused the church's awareness of the need for trained women to share in this task which to a large extent lay outside the abilities and opportunities of the male clergy.

In 1872, Mrs. Lucy Rider Meyer, a well-educated young woman, conceived the idea of a school to train young women for services for which the church felt a responsibility. In October 1885 the Chicago Training School welcomed its first class. Three years later, in 1888, the General Conference of The Methodist Episcopal Church recognized the school as a part of its church polity and authorized the office of deaconess in the church.

From 1880 through the early decades of the twentieth century, Methodist women rallied to assume responsibility and leadership in extending and strengthening the witness of the church through educational, social welfare, and medical agencies, as well as the local parish. The idea of women serving the church on a full-time basis spread through the country. After a spirited discussion, the General Conference of The Methodist Episcopal Church, South, established the office of deaconess and its first five deaconesses were consecrated in 1903. The Methodist Protestant Church, a third branch of this denominational body which became divided during the period of the Civil War, authorized the office of deaconess in 1908.

Within the United Evangelical tradition, deaconess service was organized in the German Conference of the Evangelical Association as early as 1874 and for the whole church in 1903. The United Brethren in Christ authorized deaconess service at their 1897 General Conference.

Through all the streams of history that have formed The United Methodist Church, deaconesses have demonstrated the ecumenical commitment of the denomination through active roles in the founding and continuing program of the World Federation of Diaconal Associations and Sisterhood (DIAKONIA) and through regional organizations, such as Diakonia of the Americas and Caribbean (DOTAC).

Through the pioneering efforts of the Methodist deaconesses, extensive programs were initiated involving the creation and development of social welfare institutions related to the church including homes for children; community centers and settlement houses in growing and congested areas; hospitals, schools, and work among minority groups and people in isolated rural and mountainous communities. In addition, deaconesses were an integral part of the staffs of local churches in urban and rural areas, assisting the pastor in the development of leadership among persons in the congregations and in various aspects of Christian education and community outreach.

Today, deaconesses are very much at the forefront of campaigns to address issues affecting the lives of people.

The Deaconess Program office represents the deaconess relationship and maintains a community of professionally competent lay women who are available to serve through The United Methodist Church. The Committee on Deaconess Service is an advisory committee to the Deaconess Program Office which has the responsibility for recommending programs for the promotion and interpretation of the Office of Deaconess, possible new fields of service, and new approaches to meet the needs of the present day. It recommends policies and procedures regarding the administration of the Office of Deaconess as it relates to various boards and agencies of the church and recommends standards pertaining to personnel practices.

There are also strong deaconess organizations in the central conferences of the Philippines and Europe who continue to respond to the problems of poverty, hunger, homelessness, unemployment/ underemployment and other injustices that call for new approaches to meet such needs and new fields of service.

(Resource material about the deaconess was provided for this article by the General Board of Global Ministries.)

The Consecrated Lay Worker

As the Evangelical United Brethren Church and the Methodist Church were becoming The United Methodist Church, the office of Lay Worker came into being. Both churches had been certifying "specialists" of various kinds for some years, but the General Conference moved toward a clearer recognition of specialized forms of ministry by calling for the consecration of "Lay Workers" by the bishop and the establishment of a "Conference Committee on the Lay Worker," even though it provided few guidelines by which such a committee would work. The response of the church to this office was "mild," to say the least. Unconvinced of the value of becoming a Lay Worker since its standards for preparation were the same as those already established for professional certification, a modest number of lay professionals responded and the general church was not mobilized to strengthen the office.

The Diaconal Minister

That failure was of brief concern, however, since the 1976 General Conference discontinued the office of Lay Worker and established in its stead the office of diaconal minister. This time the church established more supportive structures. Bishops were placed under mandate to appoint conference Boards of Diaconal Ministry. The general church placed the responsibility of diaconal ministry within the General Board of Higher Education and Ministry with full division status. Within three years, 900 diaconal ministers were consecrated; almost every annual conference had a functioning Board of Diaconal Ministry; and budgets allocated and inquiries about the diaconate indicated substantial interest in a servant ministry with new directions and new requirements for entrance.

Opening new possibilities for varieties of servant ministry and thereby capturing the imaginations of "beginners," as well as of those seeking a second career, the concept of a renewed permanent diaconate began to take hold. Hundreds of persons across the church responded to their "call" to ministry as a profession and in keeping with their gifts chose diaconal ministry as a valid alternative to the pastoral role.

The majority of diaconal ministers were Christian educators and musicians. Church administrators, evangelists, church communicators, church and community workers, professors of Christian education, counselors, local church program directors, age-level specialists, health care personnel, and many other emerging forms of service made up diaconal ministry.

But it was only a beginning. The 1980 General Conference established diaconal ministry as one of two forms of "representative" ministry in the church. Diaconal ministers were called to represent or "present again" the ministry of Jesus Christ to the congregation and to the world.

The Ordained Deacon in Full Connection

"From the earliest days of the church, deacons were called and set apart for the ministry of love, justice, and service; of connecting the church with the most needy, neglected, and marginalized among the children of God. This ministry grows out of the Wesleyan passion for social holiness and ministry among the poor." (¶328, *Discipline*)

The ministry of the 21st century ordained deacon in full connection has been taking shape since 1968 when the church began appointing commissions to study ministry at the merger of the Evangelical United Brethren Church and the Methodist Church. You've read above about the emergence of the office of consecrated lay worker from 1968 and the office of consecrated diaconal minister from 1976.

In 1992, the commission to study ministry's amended report to General Conference recommended a permanent ordained deacon who would be non-itinerating, and a clergy member of the annual conference, ordained to liturgy and service. This recommended report was referred to the Council of Bishops for a holistic study of ministry for four more years.

Out of that study came a recommendation to the 1996 General Conference from the Council of Bishops and the momentous decision for a permanent order of ordained deacon in full connection. The deacon in full connection is non-itinerating but appointed by the bishop in consultation with the deacon and the place of service. The deacon is appointed to a local church as well as any other place of service; this becomes a secondary appointment for those who are serving in appointments beyond the local church. Educational requirements for the deacon in full connection are equivalent of a Master of Divinity degree but allow flexibility as to an educational track that fit the person's specialized calling. The distinct calling of both the deacon and elder are expressed in two separate, equal ordinations and orders: the deacon is ordained to a lifetime ministry of Word and Service; the elder is ordained to a lifetime ministry of Word, Sacrament, Order, and Service.

The charge of the deacon in full connection is to help the church reach a new consciousness of the needs of the world and equip the church to respond effectively to those needs in fulfilling the call to servant ministry of all baptized Christians.

The Ministry of the Elder in Methodism

To understand the ministry of the elder in Methodism, it is important to go back to the roots of the movement and the assumptions which undergirded it. Methodism, in its earliest form, was essentially a lay movement **within** the Church of England, and Methodists were expected to continue under the care of the Anglican priest. John Wesley would have seen any ordination as a contradiction, since he relied on the Anglican priesthood for sacramental ministry and ordained leadership. He raised up class leaders and preachers for the work of revival and assumed the ordination of deacon and *presbyteros* (presbyter, priest, or elder). This process "entailed, after the attainment of a Bachelor of Arts degree, examination under the bishop prior to ordination as a deacon, then, after two years of probation in that status, another examination under the bishop and ordination as a presbyter or priest" (Heitzenrater, Richard P., *Wesley and the People Called Methodist*, Nashville: Abingdon Press, p. 33). John Wesley was ordained a deacon in 1725, served as a curate with his father in Epworth, and was ordained a presbyter (priest) on September 22, 1728.

Ministry in The Early Methodist Movement

Since early Methodism put its primary emphasis on preaching, Wesley was not initially concerned about ordination for his preachers. Instead, he relied on God to raise up servants with the necessary gifts to communicate the gospel—servants who had a special call to preach. For those who claimed such a call, Wesley developed a process whereby the call and the gifts could be examined before a person was authorized to travel the circuits and preach in the Methodist societies.

Because of Wesley's emphasis on the special call of God to preach, his insistence that the Methodist Societies remain in a relationship with the Church of England, and his conviction that Methodists should receive the rites and sacraments of the church from an Anglican priest, Methodism was able to continue as a religious revival within the Church of England without an ordained ministry. This proved to be an effective strategy for the Wesleyan movement until Methodism began to spread beyond the shores of England. Then, because of the scarcity or absence of Anglican clergy in America, Ireland, Scotland, and even remote areas of England, Wesley became aware that the plan for ministry needed to be changed.

Wesley's view of ordination went through a series of changes during his life. He began with the belief that Episcopal ordination was necessary for both the validity of sacraments and authority in preaching. In the 1740's and 1750's, however, he became convinced that while ordination was not necessary for preaching, it was necessary for the administration of the sacraments. His preachers, therefore, could function with full authority to proclaim the word without ordination. About the same time, Wesley also became convinced that the orders of priests and bishops were essentially the same, only functionally different, and that the New Testament did not prescribe a particular form of church order or government. As an ordained "presbyter" or elder, Wesley came to believe that he had the right to ordain. Though he did not immediately find it necessary to do so, he believed he could ordain to a ministry of Word and Sacrament.

The growth of Methodism to the American continent and Wesley's view of his functional authority as a "New Testament bishop" led to a fundamental change in the practice of ministry. Anglican clergymen were few and far between as a result of the Revolution, and the few that remained were inadequate to meet the need. With the westward expansion of the nation and the absence of Anglican clergy on the frontier, the need for ordained preachers forced Wesley to act. His diary says that he "appointed" Richard Whatcoat and Thomas Vasey "to go and serve the desolate sheep in America." They were, in fact, ordained elders by Wesley. His diary also says that he "ordained" Thomas Coke as superintendent for America. These moves had a significant impact on Methodism in America, an impact which has given shape and form to our present understanding of elder.

By acceding to the need for ordination, and by including in his Sunday Service for American Methodists a set of prescribed ordination rituals for the "orders" of deacons, elders, and superintendents, Wesley did in fact lay the groundwork for the transformation of Methodism from a lay movement to a clerical church. His lay preachers eventually came to regard themselves as "ministers," but as long as he lived, Wesley rejected their use of this term, preferring instead to use the term "preacher." He was horrified at Asbury and others whom he had sent to America as "superintendents," but who then called themselves "bishops." Nevertheless, both Wesley himself and the developing church in America contributed to the break from the Anglican model of ordained ministry and the move toward present-day patterns.

When the Christmas Conference 1784 gave birth to a new church, independent from the Church of England, they adopted the

Anglican model of ordination and Frances Asbury was ordained deacon, then elder, and named as the first bishop of the new church. This new church combined the understanding of ordination from its Anglican roots with the revivalist zeal of the lay preacher, but the basic understanding of ordained ministry as apostolic and sacramental with persons being ordained deacon for a time of probation and then ordained elder (instead of presbyter or priest) remained for 200 years.

The extensive use of laypersons as preachers, class leaders, and exhorters continued to be the evangelistic strategy which propelled the spread of Methodism throughout the new nation. The natural outgrowth of this dependence on lay leadership was the practice of ordaining licensed local preachers so that congregations could have sacramental ministry through an ordained person. As early as 1798, a local preacher could be ordained as a "local deacon" after preaching for four years. With four years of additional experience and satisfactory progress in the Course of Study, local deacons could be ordained as "local elders." This made it possible for many small churches to be assigned an ordained minister with full sacramental authority. It continued in the Methodist Episcopal and then the Methodist Church until the creation of The United Methodist Church in 1968 when the possibility of ordaining a person as a local elder rather than a traveling elder in full connection was removed from the Book of Discipline in favor of receiving associate members into the clergy membership and ordaining them as permanent deacons.

The Elder Today

Today, The United Methodist Church looks at ordination in the context of the ministry of God incarnate in the ministry of Jesus Christ and embodied in the church, the people of God. The *Book of Discipline* states the following:

> ¶301.2. *Within the church community, there are persons whose gifts, evidence of God's grace, and promise of future usefulness are affirmed by the community, and who respond to God's call by offering themselves in leadership as ordained ministers.*

Though called to a distinct ministry by God and the church, the ordained elder's ministry is never separate from the ministry of the whole people of God. Elders are ordained within the ministry of the whole church to a lifetime ministry of Service, Word, Sacrament, and Order and are authorized to preach and teach the Word of God, to administer the sacraments, to order the church for mission, and administer the Discipline. The elder leads the people of God in worship and prayer, leads persons to faith in Jesus Christ, and exercises pastoral supervision in the congregation.

Through the ordination to "sacrament," the elder continues to carry the responsibility for the sacramental ministry of the church. The elder is also ordained to "order," meaning that the elder assumes the task of overseeing the mission and ministry of the church and shares with the bishop the task of administration of the *Discipline*. For this reason, bishops and district superintendents are chosen from those who are ordained to this ministry of "ordering the life of the church for its mission and ministry." The elder shares with the deacon the ordination to Word and Service since all ordination is related to the apostolic task and the call to servant leadership in the church and the world.

Through 200 years of Methodist history, and reaching back into the Anglo/Catholic roots of our church, the elder represents the continuity of apostolic and sacramental ministry in the life of the church.

Appendix C

The United Methodist Church Course of Study

The Course of Study is a basic theological education program of the Division of Ordained Ministry. It is provided for those who are licensed as local pastors and who are not attending an approved seminary. Participants in the program should have completed the process for certified candidacy with the district committee on ordained ministry, completed the studies for license as a local pastor, and been approved for license by the dCOM.

The Course of Study is offered at regional Course of Study schools each summer on the campuses of several United Methodist theological seminaries. Most courses are offered in a two-week module that allows both full-time and part-time local pastors to attend. Many of the regional schools have extension centers for part-time local pastors only. These extension centers usually offer courses in a two- or three-weekend format which allows bi-vocational local pastors to participate without taking time away from their work or family. Students who are unable to attend any of these schools may, with the permission of the Board of Ordained Ministry, take their courses through the correspondence curriculum provided by the Division of Ordained Ministry.

Students in the Course of Study are expected to take no more than four courses per conference year. This is to allow for adequate preparation for classes at a Course of Study school and time for the integration of learning under the supervision of a Clergy Mentor. Students are discouraged from moving through the Course of Study at a pace which does not allow for adequate preparation or integration of learnings.

Local pastors who complete the requirements of the Course of Study may continue their preparation for conference membership and ordination as an elder through an Advanced Course of Study program. The *Book of Discipline* requires that local pastors who seek ordination through advanced studies

1. complete a bachelor's degree from a college or university recognized by the University Senate, or in some instances, for missional purposes, a minimum of sixty (60) semester hours of Bachelor of Arts credit (¶ 324.3);

2. reach forty (40) years of age;

3. complete the five-year Course of Study; and

4. complete thirty-two semester hours of graduate theological study or its equivalent as determined by the General Board of Higher Education and Ministry

5. including standard courses in United Methodist doctrine, polity, and history (¶ 324.6).

A candidate may request that work completed at a recognized school of theology be evaluated by the Division of Ordained Ministry for transfer to the Course of Study curriculum. The request for the evaluation must come from the annual conference Board of Ordained Ministry and an official transcript must be supplied.

No credit is recognized in the Course of Study for work completed on the undergraduate level. However, some graduate studies in counseling, business, and education may be applied to the Course of Study, as well as a basic unit of clinical pastoral education (CPE).

The policies of the Division of Ordained Ministry allow up to three courses from a regionally accredited graduate program to be applied to the Advanced Course of Study. Graduate transcripts must be sent to the Division of Ordained Ministry for evaluation before such credit may be granted.

Seminary courses in United Methodist doctrine, polity, and history must be included in the 32 semester hours of graduate theological study required for conference membership and ordination as an elder. These courses may be taken at an approved school of theology or through the independent study program of the Division of Ordained Ministry.

Requirements for Candidates Qualifying through the Course of Study for Ordained Ministry

License as a local pastor

The studies for license as a local pastor are offered by the annual conference BOM according to guidelines developed by the Division of Ordained Ministry. The guidelines suggest a minimum total of 80 hours of study in four practical areas: Worship and Preaching, Church Administration, Christian Education, and Pastoral Care. Students who have completed one third of the work required for an M.Div. degree may be approved for license as a local pastor without completing the licensing studies provided through the annual conference.

A candidate for the license as local pastor must have

1. been graduated from an accredited high school or its equivalent;
2. been a member in good standing of the recommending local United Methodist church for a minimum of two years immediately preceding the application for candidacy, including a year of service in some form of congregational leadership;
3. read *The Christian as Minister* and completed *A Ministry Inquiry Process* (recommended, but not required);
4. explored candidacy for ordained ministry with a candidacy mentor;
5. received the recommendation of his/her local charge conference; and
6. completed the process of certification for candidacy with the dCOM (¶311.1-4).

Local Pastor

A local pastor is approved annually by the dCOM and licensed by the bishop to perform all the duties of a pastor (¶316), including the sacraments of baptism and Holy Communion. The authority is granted for one year at a time under the appointment of the bishop and cabinet and under the supervision of a clergy mentor. All local pastors have been certified as candidates and have completed the studies for the license as a local pastor before being eligible for appointment (¶315-316).

The categories of local pastor are:

A. Full-time Local Pastors (¶ 318.1)

1. devote their entire time to the charge to which they are appointed;
2. receive in cash support per annum a sum equal to minimum base compensation established by the annual conference for full-time local pastors;
3. unless they have completed the Course of Study, shall complete four courses per year;
4. shall complete the Course of Study curriculum within eight years;
5. when they have completed the Course of Study, are involved in continuing education;
6. are subject to annual conference review by district committee,

cabinet, and board of ordained ministry; and

7. are clergy members of the annual conference while under appointment.

B. Part-time Local Pastors (¶ 318.2)

1. do not devote their entire time to the charge to which they are appointed;
2. do not receive in cash support per annum a sum equal to minimum base compensation;
3. unless they have completed the Course of Study, shall complete two courses per year;
4. shall complete the Course of Study curriculum within twelve years;
5. are subject to annual conference review by district committee, cabinet, and board of ordained ministry; and
6. are clergy members of the annual conference while under appointment.

C. Student Local Pastors (¶ 318.3):

1. are enrolled as pretheological or theological students in a college, university, or school of theology listed by the University Senate;
2. make appropriate progress in their educational program as determined by the board of ordained ministry;
3. are subject to annual conference review by the board of ordained ministry;
4. are not clergy members; and
5. have voice but no vote in the annual conference session.

Course of Study Schools

The Course of Study schools are held for one month each summer on the campuses of the following United Methodist seminaries:

Candler School of Theology – Emory University
Course of Study School for Local Pastors
Atlanta, GA 30322
Phone 404/737-4587; Fax 404/727-6582
cos@learnlink.emory.edu
Web site: www.candler.emory.edu/academic/cos

Claremont School of Theology
Course of Study/Licensing School
1325 N. College Ave.

Claremont, CA 91711
909/447-2573 or 909/447-2582
Web site: www.cst.edu/academic_resources/cslslp.php

Duke University Divinity School
Course of Study for Ordained Ministry
312 Blackwell St., Suite 101
Durham, NC 27701
Phone 919/613-5323; Fax 919/613-5333
Web site: www.divinity.duke.edu/learningforlife/programs/cos

Garrett-Evangelical Theological School
Course of Study School
2121 Sheridan Road
Evanston, IL 60201
847/866-3861
Web site: www.garrett.edu/menu.asp?A=4

Methodist Theological School in Ohio
Course of Study of Ohio
3081 Columbus Pike
Delaware, OH 43015
Phone 740/362-3120
cos@mtso.edu
Web site: www.courseofstudyschoolofohio.com

Perkins School of Theology - Southern Methodist University
Course of Study School
P.O. Box 750133
Dallas, TX 75275
Phone 214/768-2768
Web site: http://smu.edu/theology/public_progs/coss/ENG/coss_eng_main.html

Saint Paul School of Theology
Course of Study School
5123 E. Truman Rd.
Kansas City, MO 64127
Phone 816/245-4864
COS@spst.edu
Web site: www.spst.edu/site/cos_students.php

Wesley Theological Seminary
4500 Mass. Ave. NW
Washington, DC 20016-5690
202/885-8688
Web site: www.wesleyseminary.edu/academics/id.17/detail.asp

Extension Centers for part-time local pastors are organized under the supervision of the director of one of the regional Course of Study schools. Information on extension centers which offer courses in a series of weekend classes may be obtained from the following schools:

Candler Course of Study School – 404/737-4587
- Alabama Course of Study Extension Center
- Appalachian Local Pastors School (ALPS)
- Candler Saturday Course of Study School
- Florida Course of Study School Extension
- Mississippi Course of Study School Extension
- Memphis/Tennessee/Holston COS Extension

Duke Course of Study School – 919/613-5323
- Duke Course of Study Weekend School

Garrett Course of Study School – 847/866/3861
- Indiana Area Course of Study School Extension
- Upper Midwest Course of Study School Extension

MTSO, Course of Study of Ohio – 740/362-3120
- West Virginia Course of Study
- Native American Course of Study Extension

Perkins Course of Study School – 214/768-2768
- Arkansas Course of Study School Extension
- North Texas Course of Study School Extension

Wesley Course of Study School – 202/885-8688
- Philadelphia Course of Study Extension
- Buffalo Course of Study School Extension

Course of Study Correspondence Curriculum

Students in the Course of Study may do their work in correspondence with the DOM when circumstances prevent them from attending a regional school in the extension program for part-time local pastors. They also may take Internet courses online. Enrollment in the correspondence or online courses must be approved by the annual conference BOM using Form #110, which may be secured at www.gbhem.org/ls-cos. Students may enroll for one to four courses in a given year and, if available, may choose to do their work online. The fee for the correspondence work is $75 per course and $125 per course for work done online. The tuition fee does not include the cost of the textbooks.

When enrollment application has been received by the DOM, the student will be sent a study guide for work done by correspondence. The study guide contains assignments for each unit, study suggestions, and directions for preparing the reports. If the student chooses to do the work online, further instructions will be sent to the student by e-mail.

Work done by correspondence or online is graded by United Methodist seminary faculty or adjunct faculty. The routine handling and grading of correspondence requires approximately four weeks. Work done online will be graded by the instructors as the student progresses through the course. A final report will be submitted to the DOM once all online assignments are done. The student has twelve months to complete the course.

Information on the Course of Study correspondence curriculum and official transcripts of the Course of Study program are available through the DOM:

Course of Study Office
Division of Ordained Ministry
P.O. Box 340007
Nashville, TN 37203-0007
Telephone: 615-340-7416
Fax: 615-340-7377
E-mail: ldaye@gbhem.org

Appendix D

Hazards in Licensed and Ordained Ministry

Licensed and Ordained Ministry: A Public Ministry

Temptations to professional misconduct are a hazard to those serving in the public ministry of the licensed and ordained. Perhaps the most classic reports of temptation and testing are contained in the drama of Job (Job 1-42, entire book) and in Matthew 4:1-11/Luke 4:1-14. Jesus coped with hazards and temptations, even up to his crucifixion (Mark 15 and its parallels).

Because licensed and ordained ministers are highly visible, their professional and personal conduct is often interpreted by persons within the church, and especially those from outside the church, as the way United Methodists (or Christians) are, or act, or do things. Licensed and ordained ministers represent and reflect the church to others, both within and outside the congregation and denomination.

Holistic and Holy Awareness

Licensed or ordained ministers' actions and lifestyle have great impact on others, often without the awareness of the clergyperson. You can become aware of your own strengths and areas for growth through prayer and discernment, including confidential conversations with your mentor, feedback from your psychological assessment, and candid comments from others who know you well and/or observe your work.

Applying the General Rules to Today's Hazards

John Wesley gave three general rules to the people called Methodists:

1. do no harm,
2. do all the good you can,
3. attend upon the ordinances of God

¶103, *Discipline*

Although specific examples have changed across the generations of Methodists, these principles apply to all of the hazards of licensed and ordained ministry.

Specific Risks and Hazards

It is easy to acknowledge these dynamics generally for all licensed and ordained ministers as a group, yet it is usually difficult to examine your own personal fitness for licensed or ordained ministry candidly and without reservation. As you review each of these conditions, keep in mind that they are actually symptoms of underlying needs. They are attempts to obtain the nurture and support you need, but the inadequate solution results in more harm and further blocks getting to the real core needs, conflicts, and problems. It is far better to cope with these now than to spend time and energy repressing, avoiding, or secretly indulging these conditions across the years of a licensed or ordained ministry crippled with fears and pain.

Stress, Strain, and Burnout

Burnout has been known to the faithful as far back as the Old Testament writings (Moses in Exodus 19; Elijah in 1 Kings 19:9-18; Jonah 1-4). Burnout may be a special danger for those who do not try to balance active service with spiritual formation and renewal. Most dedicated persons, including licensed and ordained ministers, work long and hard to improve some aspect of the world. With high goals and intense effort you may become disheartened when others do not share your goals, seem less enthusiastic about them, or thwart your best efforts. Administrative disagreements, lack of budget funding, shortage of committed persons, and increased numbers of needy persons can contribute to burnout.

Some stress is normal and to be expected in licensed and ordained ministry. Too much stress strains your system beyond its ability to cope, resulting in burnout, depression, and/or other serious reactions that remove you from the stressors.

The burnout syndrome usually includes feeling frustrated, angry, exhausted, abandoned, and/or unsupported. Irritability, bitterness, aggression, and fatigue also appear, often leading to a sense of defeat and inadequacy that can lead to depression.

Jesus reminded his disciples to "come away and rest for a while" (Mark 6:30-31). Being effective in licensed and ordained ministry means that you also have developed appropriate self-care habits that recreate and refresh you. "R and R" time is not wasted time when it is in the service of renewing you for the work ahead.

Now is the time for you to check your patterns of self-care that will prevent burnout and other serious consequences of too much stress. Your system of self-care may include family resources, peer support groups, regular self-assessment of your stress versus strain ratio in relation to your resources for recovery, retreat times, and professional consultation or therapy.

List your disciplines or methods for self-care by which you cope with your own potential burnout.

Depression

Depression literally reduces (depresses) your ability to respond to life, usually because you think that whatever responses you might make are unacceptable, inadequate, will be rejected, or will cause more trouble. Depression is like an emotional and spiritual cold that takes you out of stressful conflicts.

Depression is a normal defense against being overcome by life. For a relatively healthy person, depression is a warning sign to get broader perspective on life events, retreat for renewal and reassessment, pray, consult with others, and reorganize yourself as you find constructive solutions to the situations that face you.

Prolonged depression drags you into fatigue, leaving you with greatly lowered energy because you are using so much energy keeping the lid on the underlying feelings that are feeding the depression.

Some signs of depression are inability to sleep or too much sleep, eating disorders, thoughts of suicide, chronic fatigue, intense feelings of shame or guilt, inability to do normal work, unrealistic fears, and chronic physical changes such as headaches, backaches, and muscular tension.

Depression may result from external situations or from changes in your body biochemistry. A tendency to depression may be your body-mind-spirit's way of alerting you to stresses you may not have otherwise noticed. As a special sensitivity of your personal system, depression may be an early warning sign that invites you to seek treatment and take needed action.

Note ways depression is or may become a danger to your calling and licensed or ordained ministry.

Addiction to work (workaholic) vs. aversion to work

In licensed and ordained ministry there is always more work to be done than a person can complete. Every licensed and ordained minister could study more, pray more, organize and lead more, visit parishioners more, and reach out to the needy and unchurched more. God calls you to the challenge of licensed and ordained ministry and asks your total commitment and energy for the work at hand. On top of normal work loads, emergencies, crises, and seasonal emphases call for additional efforts.

Responses to the work load of licensed and ordained ministry may go either to one extreme of overwork or the other extreme of underwork.

Time for licensed and ordained ministry must be balanced with time for family, rest, and renewal. Licensed and ordained ministers must balance these elements in ways that fit both their effectiveness in their work and their personal commitments to renewal and family. Exactly what an appropriate balance should be varies in many ways.

Overwork: Some persons may respond to the challenges of licensed and ordained ministry by becoming addicted to their work or workaholic. Persons may spend most of their waking hours doing the work of licensed and ordained ministry. Work becomes an addiction when a person cannot turn loose of it or feels compelled to continue work far beyond normal expectations.

The Protestant work ethic, the satisfaction from doing a job well, having your accomplishments recognized by others, and other factors may unintentionally encourage a person toward work addiction.

Feelings of inadequacy or guilt, lack of good management skills, and mistrust of others may contribute to chronic addiction to overwork.

What are your expectations about the normal work load and weekly work hours for you as a licensed and ordained minister?

Underwork: Other persons respond to the challenges of licensed and ordained ministry by avoiding work or by doing just enough to get by. While overwork can be valued by society, doing less than is expected (underwork) carries stigmas of being lazy, lax, and uncommitted to Christ's calling.

Among factors that may lead to underwork are a lack of skill, fear of conflict, poor time management, demands from family, low energy, depression, feelings of inadequacy or failure, addictions, and misperceptions of oneself or of the job requirements.

In what ways might you try to avoid doing appropriate work requirements or expectations?

Sexual Misconduct

Sexual testings and temptations to misconduct come in many varieties. The mass media portrays so many varieties of inappropriate sexual conduct so often that they may seem normal and desirable. In the church, extramarital sexual involvements and inappropriate sexual contacts between a licensed or ordained minister and his or her parishioners are obvious types of sexual misconduct.

God created sexuality as a powerful channel for love, affirmation, and reproduction that helps to validate you, increase self-esteem, and confirm you in your identity before God. Like all God-given powers, licensed and ordained ministers can misuse sexuality in ways that harm others as well as themselves, destroying the ministries of many.

Continuing effectiveness in licensed and ordained ministry insists that both you and the church maintain a healthy sexuality that allows you to serve professionally, comfortably, and safely with persons of both genders and all ages. A guide for sexual wholeness is provided in the Book of Discipline:

> *. . . to exercise responsible self-control by personal habits conducive to bodily health, mental and emotional maturity, integrity in all personal relationships, fidelity in marriage and celibacy in singleness, . . .(¶ 324.9o).*

How do you apply this guide in your life?

Since licensed and ordained ministers are entrusted with the care of persons who are often most vulnerable to sexual overtones from those in authority, it is especially important that persons entering licensed and ordained ministry are clear about the power differential in ministerial relationships and their own sexual boundaries, and are able to build trust and openness in the Christian fellowship.

Some examples of sexual misconduct are sexual abuse of children or anyone else, pornography, overt or covert romantic contacts with parishioners, sexual addictions, sexual harassment, and giving preferences to selected persons because of their sexual attractiveness or flirtations.

It is appropriate for those who evaluate your promise for effectiveness in licensed or ordained ministry to look carefully for any signs of physical violence against others, sexual acting out, sexual abuse from you to others, and related activities that could potentially bring harm to others from you.

Persons who want the finest for licensed or ordained ministry welcome honest inquiry concerning these difficult areas, but persons who avoid such personal questions may have something to hide or may need to address feelings about potential conflicts or harmful activities.

In what ways might your sexual behaviors become a problem for you or for the church? How will (or do) you cope with these before they damage others or yourself?

Authority

Relationships with official authorities confront licensed and ordained ministers in many ways. As a licensed or ordained minister, you must accept the authority of others, such as your district superintendent, bishop, and the elected and appointed lay leaders in your congregation. You also may exercise authority over others in the parish and community because of your role as a licensed or ordained minister. Education and supervision relationships also have authority dimensions.

In relation to appropriate authorities you may be overly dependent, passive, and compliant, or you may be overly controlling, demanding, and noncooperative. You may be too eager to please those over you, whatever the cost to you because you are afraid you may lose their favor or support. On the other hand, you may not respect authority or may openly or passively try to avoid or subvert their appropriate directions to you.

The connectional system of The United Methodist Church brings both advantages and disadvantages. It requires licensed and ordained ministers who are sufficiently assertive and energetic to serve effectively, yet are able to work within the hierarchical structure of the denomination.

One danger facing our denomination today may be that candidates who are sufficiently independent and talented to move rapidly into leadership positions may become frustrated with the many details and complexities of the bureaucratic structure and leave our denomination for other church settings that seem to have fewer administrative blocks and hassles.

When energetic persons with many talents do not enter licensed and ordained ministry, by default it may leave the church with candidates who are more passive, less talented, and less able to lead the denomination in the continuing renewal that is essential for future effective and creative ministries.

Personal management and finances

Personal management and mismanagement include how you manage your own time, personal finances, and home. "Are you in debt so as to embarrass you in your work?" (*Discipline*, ¶336.18) extends also to mismanaging your own finances in ways that embarrass or harm the licensed or ordained ministry of the church. Excessive debts and failure to pay back debts or pay taxes are also examples of mismanagement, as are borrowing without intending to repay and using one's influence as a licensed or ordained minister for personal gain.

Effectiveness means that you manage, and will continue to learn to manage, your own household, including your finances well. (I Timothy 3:4) John Wesley urged his followers to "gain all you can, save all you can, give all you can" with equal emphasis on all three directives, not just the first. Good financial management implies dealing with whatever greed may be in you.

Honesty in your own stewardship of your finances and time suggests that you can use these attitudes and experiences as you are involved in the stewardship of church funds and programs.

Financial integrity and management also includes your decisions about gambling, lottery, and other forms of chance that promise something for nothing. United Methodists have long opposed all forms of gambling for many reasons (see Social Principles, ¶¶160-66, *Discipline*).

The increased use of gambling to produce additional funds for good causes, such as schools and government operations, suggests that the end justifies the means, a principle that is opposed to the highest Christian views of money, time, and resources.

The publicity given to lottery winners obscures the hundreds of thousands of persons who took money from limited family budgets and bet it against overwhelming odds that they would lose. These pressures push some farther toward gambling addictions.

Note personal and financial issues that affect you.

Substance Abuse

Alcoholism and/or other substance abuse is widespread in society. United Methodists seek both to contain and stop the social causes of substance abuse as well as to offer Christian treatment to those who become dependent on alcohol or other drugs or food.

Some licensed and ordained ministers may be caught in the web of substance abuse but may avoid confronting their addiction. We celebrate those who have obtained treatment and are in recovery. As you consider your own fitness for licensed or ordained ministry, examine also whether you might become emotionally dependent upon alcohol and/or other drugs, medications, food, or other substances that would hinder your effectiveness as a licensed or ordained minister and as a Christian.

Note your personal responses to substance abuse issues.

Violence and Abuse

Abuse may be verbal, physical, and/or sexual. Neglect and abandonment are also forms of abuse. Trauma from accidents, unexpected deaths, or natural disasters may also continue to affect you today.

Abuse and trauma, whether past or present, may affect our fitness for licensed or ordained ministry if you have not satisfactorily addressed its impact on your life now and in the future.

You may also experience current or recent abuse from sexual harassment, prejudiced employer or employee biases, and other sources that impact your approach to licensed or ordained ministry. In reaction, you may either overlook the abuse or retaliate against others when you have opportunity to do so. Both extremes mean that you may still need to work through the abusive or traumatic experiences in relation to your fitness for licensed or ordained ministry.

Note ways in which violence and abuse may be issues for you.

Some Concluding Thoughts

Considering these hazards and dangers may sound like a legalistic approach to preparation and effectiveness for licensed or ordained ministry. Like the Ten Commandments, a code of ethics for licensed and ordained ministers can be a guide or a schoolmaster to you as a Christian who seeks to live by faith in the grace of God. You ignore these possible pitfalls at the peril of yourself as well as the church both present and future.

Healthy fitness for licensed and ordained ministry crowds out negatives like those considered in this guide. A constant growth in love and grace brings a firm foundation from which you can invite the Holy Spirit to confront your vulnerabilities and nurture you into greater wholeness and fitness for licensed or ordained ministry.

Issues of the proper use of power and authority are behind most of the dangers and hazards of licensed and ordained ministry. As you consider potential pitfalls you might face, try to identify how they may be related to underlying feelings of inadequacy, rejection, or abandonment. Often misuse of power is motivated by an individual's need for acceptance, nurture, and recognition. In your own spiritual searching try to trace the motivations that underlie behaviors that hurt others and yourself.

Maintaining healthy fitness requires your own plan for self-care. With your candidacy mentor consider how your self-care patterns address the hazards and dangers of licensed and ordained ministry that you may encounter. He or she can also help you develop and enlarge your self-care patterns should you need that.

Record your plan for spiritual disciplines of self-care here (e.g., reading a book, taking a walk, etc.).

Appendix E

Excerpts from Understanding God's Call:
A Ministry Inquiry Process
Calling Through Healing, Teaching, and Sending

(Excerpts from *Ministry Inquiry Process*, session 2: "The Bible and God's Call")

Calling

"Calling" is when someone gets your attention and engages you in a relationship. The name you call someone else establishes a relationship that identifies both you and the other person. To call "Hey, you!" is different from calling you by either an affectionate or a derogatory name.

Your parents or significant caregivers called you by name when you were a young child. Later you chose either to accept that name or change it in some way, perhaps using different nicknames according to the different groups in which you were involved.

Calling comes out of a relationship with God. In Scripture, calling is when God initially reaches out to a person or group. Sometimes God calls in very dramatic and unexpected ways, and at other times God calls in quiet, routine, or predictable experiences.

The Gospels describe how Jesus called the twelve disciples or apostles to go and serve (Mark 3:13-19, Matthew 10:1-4, Luke 6:12-16). There are many other instances when Jesus invited his followers to come to him.

God's Call in the Bible

With your guide, read and discuss one or more of these biblical examples of calling:

Old Testament
- Jacob, Genesis 32:22-32
- Esther, Esther 4
- Isaiah, Isaiah 6
- Jeremiah, Jeremiah 1:4-19
- Ezekiel, Ezekiel 1-3

New Testament
- Zechariah and Elizabeth, Luke 1
- Mary, Luke 1
- John the Baptist, Luke 3:1-20
- Timothy, 2 Timothy 3:10-4:5
- Disciples, Mark 3:13-19, Matthew 10:1-4, Luke 6: 12-16

1. How does God's call come to the persons involved?

2. How does each person respond? To what extent is each person confident, hesitant, willing, or uncertain? How does each person feel about her/his call?

3. In your New Testament example, talk about the ways God in Christ offers healing and reassurance to the person called.

4. To what task is each called? How do these tasks differ among the persons called at different times?

God's Call in Your Life

1. What are some other examples of God's callings that you have experienced or heard about?

2. God's call to you is your special invitation to respond. Calling happens when you feel drawn, attracted, compelled, fascinated, or curious about something. Something or someone has your attention. The next task is to discover who has called you and why.
   a. Describe some ways you are aware of God's calling you.

   b. What insights and discoveries from your study of biblical call help you understand your own experience?

God's Call through the Sacraments

God calls you through the sacraments of Baptism and the Lord's Supper. These serve as reminders of God's grace in the very basic human experiences of birth, naming, meals, and other experiences of physical and spiritual nurture in your family or in other close relationships—both growing up and currently.

1. Tell the story of your baptism. How does God call you through your baptism?

2. Recall a memorable time at the Lord's Table. How does God call you through Communion?

Reflection

- Do I desire to hear and do God's will?

- Do I want to live a life aligned with God's will for me, regardless of where that commitment will take me?

- Am I going to trust God with my future?

Healing

The Holy Spirit helps you hear God's call through healing. Healing may be needed to overcome obstacles that keep you from responding to God's calling. Healing gives you the eyes and ears of faith so you can understand God's teachings, receive the nurture of the Holy Spirit, and respond to God's call.

There are many terms or metaphors for your spiritual being that God heals such as will, heart, motivation, attitude, mind, depths of being, and right relationship. All of these are helpful, yet none of the terms fully describes the awe and mystery of the Holy Spirit's indwelling and healing.

What does the word "healing" mean to you?

Calling and Healing in the Bible

Jesus said that he has come to heal those who are sick or bound by sin (see Luke 5:31-32). When you are healed by God through the

Holy Spirit, your relationship with God is restored. You are aware that God loves you, is continually seeking to be reconciled with you, and is calling you to go and serve.

1. Note the many instances of Jesus' healing others.

2. How did the persons respond to the healing?

Calling and Healing in Your Life

Because Christians value physical healing in all its forms, physical healing serves as a metaphor pointing to the work of the Holy Spirit in changing heart or attitude, bringing wholeness. Healing helps you to be open to God's calling through teaching and nurture and then to go out in Christ's name to serve others.

1. Describe some of the ways you have experienced God's healing grace in your life.

2. How does the Holy Spirit open you to discerning God's call in your own life journey?

Reflection

- What must I lay down and what must I take up in order to go forward with God without pre-judgment about what the direction will be or must be for me?

- What healing do I need in order to live in union of faith and love with God?

Teaching

In the Gospels, accounts of Jesus' healing of one or more persons are usually followed with a parable, teaching, or interpretation. God calls persons to serve through teaching as preparation for being sent into the world.

Jesus' teaching in the Sermon on the Mount in Matthew 5-7 and Luke 6 assumes that people are able to see, hear, receive, and understand the Gospel. The Gospel calls people to live in God's way.

Calling and Teaching in the Bible

Read Matthew 5:1-12 and talk with your guide about what Jesus was trying to teach those who were present through the Beatitudes.

1. What do the Beatitudes tell you about what it means to live in God's way (phrases beginning with "Blessed are . . .")?

2. What is promised to those who live in God's way (phrases beginning with "for they . . .")?

3. How is God calling persons through Jesus' teaching in the Beatitudes?

4. How would you share the meaning of the Beatitudes in your own words?

List some of Jesus' teachings that are especially significant for you. What do they teach you about God's calling and living in God's way?

Calling and Teaching in Your Life

Teaching and healing interact, nurturing both the receiver and the giver in many ways. God's healing restores persons to wholeness and brings reconciliation to relationships. Reconciliation helps both teacher and hearer see and hear by faith—to hear God's calling.

Think of one person whose life has affected you in important ways.

1. In what ways has God's calling through healing and teaching been a part of this relationship?

2. What have you learned from this person?

3. How did this person nurture you and help give you a glimpse of God's reign?

Describe some of your own teaching and nurturing abilities. How have you taught or nurtured others? How might you participate in teaching others about God's way?

Reflection

- What are the possible directions God is calling me and that I am prompted to take?

- What are my gifts and graces?

- What are the needs that touch me?

- What may be the best possible routes for me, given my gifts and graces?

Sending

Going out to serve in the world is a response to God's calling, but sending may also be a vehicle for God's call. In the going and serving, you may hear a further call.

Calling and Sending in the Bible

The Bible reports that Jesus calls disciples, and then through healing and teaching sends them out into the world (see Luke 10, Luke 24).

Read the Great Commission in Matthew 28:19-20. It clearly summarizes God's calling through healing, teaching, and sending disciples out into the world. What does it say to you?

An important meaning of every Christian's vocational journey is that God's calling through healing and teaching sends people out in God's service. A worship service ends by sending people into the world to serve as a healed and prepared (educated, trained) representative or disciple of Christ.

Calling and Sending in Your Life

Sending involves matching an inner call from God with an outward or external call from others for service. Discernment about how an external call to service fulfills your inner call from God will require careful assessment of your gifts and graces, listening to those who know you well, and praying for clarity to do God's will.

Answering the following questions may help you begin to clarify how God is calling you and where God is sending you. You may also revisit your own personal story and life journey to identify the talents and abilities God has given you.

1. What are some needs of the world that challenge you?

2. What are some talents, gifts, skills, abilities that you have or could develop to meet these needs?

3. Where do the needs of the world and your talents meet? How could you uniquely address the need?

4. Could you best minister to the need through a paid or volunteer position in a local church, a church agency, a parachurch or nonprofit organization, a government agency, a position in business or industry, or other paid or volunteer work?

Reflection

- As I set my preferences before God one at a time, with which do I have peace with God and sense God is sending me forward in faith?

- Which route opens the way for me to give fullest expression to my "Here am I" to the Lord and meets the human need toward which God has directed me?

Review and Closing

In the world you experience both victories and defeats. The din of other voices and forces can fatigue and temporarily overpower you. Therefore God's calling through healing, teaching, and sending begins every time God draws you back to Christ's body for healing and renewal. Daily and weekly calls to return to God's sanctuary for prayer and worship are an important way the Holy Spirit renews you for your good work in the world for God. Once renewed, the Spirit sends you out again to serve.

1. What have you learned about God's calling through healing, teaching, and sending? Enter any notes to aid you in this process.

Spiritual Practices

(Parts of Session 3 in *Understanding God's Call: A Ministry Inquiry Process*, pgs 46-52 were adapted and used in the beginning of Unit 19, "Spiritual Life. That excerpt is included here.)

Growing in your relationship to God and becoming clear about your call to licensed or ordained ministry requires careful and ongoing nurture, just as a gardener would tend a prize plant from seed to blossoming.

John Wesley, the founder of Methodism, knew that people need to cultivate their spiritual lives in community. The goal is for Christians to become more Christlike, or more holy, in their daily living and this does not happen alone. People need the company of other faithful Christians on their spiritual journeys.

1. Reflect on the spiritual practices that you have tried that have been most nurturing to your spiritual journey.

2. Your personality influences the spiritual practices that are most helpful. What changes and/or development have you experienced in your spiritual practices?

3. Talk with your mentor about how any spiritual practices have raised questions about the meaning of faith for you.

4. What is it about the spiritual practices you have used that have been helpful for your growth in faith?

Means of Grace

Specific spiritual practices or disciplines helped early Methodists cultivate their spiritual lives. These practices were called the "means of grace."

God does not abandon people on their spiritual journeys. God provides the means of grace to help people continue on the way to wholeness through a deeper relationship with God. These spiritual practices are a response to God who loved people first; they are not a way to earn God's love.

1. **Prayer.** What are the ways you pray and what are other methods of prayer that you might want to explore?

2. **Searching the Scriptures.** What are some of the different ways you have studied Scripture? How has God been revealed to you through searching the Scriptures?

3. **The Lord's Supper.** Talk about your participation in Holy Communion and what it means to your spiritual life.

4. **Fasting.** Talk about your experience with fasting as a spiritual practice. How might a person fast from something other that food?

5. **Acts of Mercy.** In what ways have you served your neighbor through acts of mercy? How has your spiritual journey been affected by service to other persons?

Ministry Options

(Excerpt from *Understanding God's Call: A Ministry Inquiry Process*, Session 9: "Ministry Options to Explore")

Servant Ministry

All Christians are called to ministry in the world. In a sense, you have an opportunity to become God's hands and feet and heart in the world through your ministry.

> *The heart of Christian ministry is Christ's ministry of outreaching love. Christian ministry is the expression of the mind and mission of Christ by a community of Christians that demonstrates a common life of gratitude and devotion, witness and service, celebration and discipleship. All Christians are called to this ministry of servanthood in the world to the glory of God and for human fulfillment. . . . (Book of Discipline, ¶125).*

Read Part III, "The Ministry of All Christians," Sections I-III, ¶¶120-132 (*Discipline*). Talk with your mentor about what the ministry of all Christians means to you.

Read Section IV in "The Ministry of All Christians" (*Discipline*, ¶¶133-135) and discuss them with your mentor.

1. What does servant ministry mean to you?

2. Review any stages of spiritual growth and transition in your own life.

3. Are the ministry of all Christians, ministry of the laity, and Christian discipleship the same? Related? How would you define each of these terms?

4. Interview a person you know who is a good role model of the ministry of all Christians. Ask questions such as: How has your relationship with God developed over your lifetime? How does being Christian affect your daily life? How are you in ministry in the world? What are the gifts of discipleship? What are the challenges?

5. If you were to continue as part of the ministry of the laity in response to God's call, how would your servant ministry be expressed through your vocation?

Servant Leadership

Read Sections V in "The Ministry of All Christians" (*Discipline*, ¶¶136-137).

Within The United Methodist Church, there are those called to servant leadership, lay and ordained. Such callings are evidenced by special gifts, evidence of God's grace, and promise of usefulness. (*Discipline*, ¶136)

1. Talk with your mentor about what servant leadership means.

2. Share your ideas about the meaning of this sentence: Ordained ministers are called by God to a lifetime of servant leadership in specialized ministries among the people of God. (¶137)

Clergy Orders

Read Sections II in "The Ministry of the Ordained" (*Discipline*, ¶¶ 310-314).

1. With your mentor, discuss the meaning of "Orders in Relation to the Ministry of all Christians," ¶310.

2. Review the purposes for an Order in ¶312. What are the advantages in belonging to an Order? Disadvantages?

The Ministry of a Deacon in Full Connection

Read ¶¶137, 328-331 in the *Discipline* about the church's understanding of "The Ministry of a Deacon."

1. Talk with your mentor about the understanding of the ministry of a deacon in these paragraphs.

2. Interview a deacon in full connection about his or her understanding of ministry. Ask questions such as: Why do you believe the ministry of a deacon in full connection is a faithful response to God's call? What kind of ministry do you have? What are the benefits of this ministry? What are the challenges? What special qualities or skills are needed for this kind of ministry?

3. If you were to enter the ministry of a deacon in response to God's call, how would your ministry be expressed through your vocation?

The Ministry of Elder

Read ¶¶137, 332-348 in the Book of Discipline about the church's understanding of "The Ministry of an Elder."

1. Talk with your mentor about the understanding of the ministry of an elder in these paragraphs.

2. Interview an elder about her or his understanding of ministry. Ask questions such as: Why do you believe the ministry of an elder is your most faithful response to God's call? What kind of ministry do you have? What are the benefits of the ministry of an elder? What are the challenges? What special qualities or skills are needed for this kind of ministry?

3. If you were to enter the ministry of an elder in response to God's call, how would your ministry be expressed through your vocation?

History of ministry orders

Read the history of the deacon and the history of the elder in Appendix B and reflect on what you have learned with your candidacy mentor.

Record questions about the history of the orders of ordained ministry here for discussion with your candidacy mentor.

Reflection with your Candidacy Mentor

Discuss the following questions with your candidacy mentor, a member of the annual conference BOM, or other ordained persons.

1. What is your understanding of ordination? How would you tell someone what it means?

2. Draw on your own experience to describe your understanding of the ministries of ordained elder, ordained deacon, and local pastor.

3. What emerging ministries are needed as we enter the twenty-first century? What roles can the ordained elder, ordained deacon, and local pastor play in these ministries?

4. How will the mission of the church to the needs of society affect the ministries of ordained elder, ordained deacon, and local pastor in the future?

5. Record other questions here for discussion with your candidacy mentor.

LaVergne, TN USA
19 March 2010
176618LV00001B/2/P